Daybreak

A Guide to Overcoming Temptation

Nathan Ward

DEWARD
PUBLISHING COMPANY

For Silas and Judah

with the prayer that they are more successful
in this endeavor than their father

CONTENTS

PREFACE

One of the first sermons I ever preached was on the topic of overcoming temptation. For a while, it was the standard "first sermon" I would preach in a new place, whether I were filling in for someone or if I had been asked to speak for a local congregation. It had four basic points: purpose purity in your heart, don't give up before the fight begins, rely on each other, and learn from your mistakes—all of which are points that you will find in the last three chapters of this book.

Over the years, I kept coming back to this sermon, probably because it is so practical and always a timely topic. It wasn't long before I added an obvious fifth point—avoid tempting situations—and the points were reorganized to a before, during, and after approach, a format it kept with only minor changes for several years.

As my thinking on the topic developed, the sermon continued to grow until that one lesson became three. From there, I added three more lessons outlining the Biblical principles that stand behind the practical points. Then came two more on getting to know the enemy.

All of that is the study from which this book was written. The course it follows is quite simple: after the introduction, I examine three aspects of our call that motivate us to overcome temptation: holiness, self-denial, and new life. From there the focus turns to the enemy: Satan and self. Finally, we turn to the practical section where we will examine basic principles of how to overcome temptation.

If it is not evident from the size of the book, this is not a comprehensive study on the topic. Much more can be and has been said. My aim, however, is not to be exhaustive but helpful—and I pray that the brief survey of these principles and practices is just that.

Nathan Ward
May 2013

INTRODUCTION

Sometimes the sun is more than just the sun and night is more than just night.

John, in his gospel, repeatedly uses light and darkness as metaphors for a spiritual condition. From the first chapter, Christ is light and all of those who are in Him are in the light. Darkness represents all that stands against God. It is no surprise, then, that John notes the time of day when Christ was betrayed. After Jesus sends Judas out, John records, "And it was night" (John 13.30). Truly, there was no night darker than that one.

In the story of Jacob, the sun is mentioned twice. First, it sets when he departs Canaan on his way to Haran (Gen 28.11). It appears again when he returns to Canaan (32.31). This sunrise bookends the sunset of chapter 28, depicting his time away from Canaan as a period of darkness. The sun had set on him as he left the Promised Land, having stolen the blessing that God intended to give him. Here, as he returns, the sun rises.

More significantly, the mention of this daybreak immediately follows Jacob's wrestling match with God where Jacob fights for a blessing and receives a new name.[1] Jacob had long been deceitful and self-sufficient. In his fight with God, Jacob is forced to acknowledge who he is. Only by doing this could he change. The sun rising represents a new day of light dawning for Jacob. Now, as a new man, he faces a new day.

As Christians, we should not live in the night. We have experienced our own daybreak and should walk in the light. But far too often, we find the darkness alluring. Perhaps we have given ourselves over to sin, lived in darkness, and are struggling to experience that daybreak again. I make no pretense about this little book being a substitute for the Bible or the illuminating power of God. But in these pages you will find some simple thoughts about overcoming temptation, and experiencing another daybreak. Join me as we consider our calling, examine our enemy, and study strategies for battle.

1

THE CALL

Holiness

Why is it so vital that we overcome temptation? We could make the simple observation that God has said not to sin, and if God has said it, that's enough. This is a legitimate argumentand properly respects the authority of God, but it may not be a sufficient answer since God has revealed more on this very topic.

It is far too easy to consider Christianity a list of rules that boils down to doing certain things or, perhaps even more likely, *not* doing certain things—that the essence of Christianity is "don't do this" and "don't do that." This misunderstanding invariably leads to a negative perception of Christianity and God. We see God as a stick-in-the-mud who doesn't want us to have any fun, with a long list of things that we can't do. In essence, we view Christianity as nothing more than prohibitions—the very same sort of mindset that we will see Satan exploit in Eve.

The reason that we need a better answer to the question of why we should overcome temptation than "God said not to sin," is that it helps reveal Satan's lie. Understanding the bigger Biblical picture shows us that God does not want to keep us from the things that will bring us pleasure, but that He alone knows what true pleasure is: fellowship with Him. God calls us to be holy because He wants us to be His people, and to be holy like Him (Lev 20.22–26).

We find this same requirement in 1 Peter, where Peter quotes God's call to holiness from Leviticus 11. Peter begins his epistle discussing the most optimistic of all topics: our living hope. It rests on the certainty of Christ's resurrection (v 3), and is an inheritance which, like the raised Christ, is incorruptible, will not fade away, and is awaiting us in heaven (v 4). This great salvation is guarded by God as we are purified by Him in anticipation of it (v 5). Just how amazing is it? Before God revealed this mystery, prophets inquired about it and angels desired to look into it (vv 9–12). This is the great hope that we have. This is the great gift God has given. This is God calling us and making us His people.

The requirement now is the same now as it was for the audience of Leviticus, who first received that calling to be God's holy people. As we live our lives in hopeful anticipation of this salvation, we are given a task: holiness. This high calling of holiness is why it is so vital that we overcome temptation.

Sin

Before turning our focus to the high calling of holiness, it is helpful to take a moment to consider the alternative: sin. We will consider our enemies in chapters four and five, but we need to look at sin from a different perspective before continuing a discussion of holiness. Part of the difficulty we face in overcoming temptation is that we do not see sin as God does. We don't see sin the way the righteous people of the Bible saw sin. We have too sanitized a view of sin.

It is easy to think poorly of Lot. After all, he chose poorly in Genesis 13 and seemed only to multiply his poor choices after that (cf. esp. Gen 19). The New Testament description of Lot, however, is of a righteous man who was greatly distressed by the sensual conduct of the wicked (2 Pet 2.7–8). We live in an eerily similar situation to Lot: surrounded by wickedness of all kinds and trying to remain pure in the midst of it all. But just how tormented are our souls over the things that we see and hear day after day? Maybe we are as tormented as we ought to be by the sin *we* commit, but we are probably not as upset over sin around us.

Why have we, who are called to such holiness, become so ambivalent toward sin? Perhaps we have bought in too much to our accepting, can't-offend-anyone culture and have come to believe that "as long as it doesn't interfere with my life, it's perfectly okay." Perhaps we have seen so much of it that we've allowed ourselves to become desensitized to sin and we shrug at it. Perhaps we have participated in so much of it that we're afraid to call it what it is. Perhaps, in excusing our own sins, we have sugar-coated it: "Everyone has faults," we say, "It's just a weakness." Whatever the case, I'm afraid that many Christians today do not see sin as God does.

If we have any hope of living up to the holiness to which we are called, we must clearly see sin. The following list is not exhaustive, but perhaps it will serve as a good starting point to grasp the reality of sin.

Sin is fighting against us. Shortly after issuing the call to holiness in chapter 1, Peter says, "I urge you as sojourners and exiles to abstain from the passions of the flesh, which wage war against your soul" (2.11). Paul also speaks of sin in this way:

> For though we walk in the flesh, we are not waging war according
> to the flesh. For the weapons of our warfare are not of the flesh but
> have divine power to destroy strongholds. We destroy arguments

and every lofty opinion raised against the knowledge of God, and take every thought captive to obey Christ, being ready to punish every disobedience, when your obedience is complete. (2 Cor 10.3–6)

Finally, be strong in the Lord and in the strength of his might. Put on the whole armor of God, that you may be able to stand against the schemes of the devil. For we do not wrestle against flesh and blood, but against the rulers, against the authorities, against the cosmic powers over this present darkness, against the spiritual forces of evil in the heavenly places. Therefore take up the whole armor of God, that you may be able to withstand in the evil day, and having done all, to stand firm. (Eph 6.10–13)

Sin is not something to wink at or shrug our shoulders at. Sin is not something to sugar-coat. Sin is not a game. Sin is a war. As is the case in any war, there is the possibility of death.

Sin is trying to kill us. From the very beginning, the result of sin has been death. God tells Adam that if he transgress the command about eating of the fruit of the tree of knowledge of good and evil, "You shall surely die" (Gen 2.17), the very promise Satan denies in chapter 3. When they eat, they are expelled from the Garden to prevent their continual life (3.22–23). The first genealogy of the Bible emphasizes the universal death of all mankind (save Enoch, ch 5). The New Testament picks up on this same principle as we are told that the wages of sin, what we earn as pay, is death (Rom 6.23). James describes the life-cycle—death-cycle, actually—of sin: "Each person is tempted when he is lured and enticed by his own desire. Then desire when it has conceived gives birth to sin, and sin when it is fully grown brings forth death" (1.14–15).

The stakes are high in spiritual warfare: it is a life and death fight. We cannot underestimate sin or look at it from our accepting culture's point of view. It is a war and our very lives are at stake.

Sin is insulting to God. It mocks the God who created us, the God who we serve, the God who saved us. When we willingly choose to go down that path, it is a slight and affront to God. The author of Hebrews makes this point especially clear as he describes the one who willfully turns his back on God after receiving the knowledge of the truth. It's a picture of someone who has a clear view of the salvation they have been offered and shrugs it off, instead living a life of self-indulgence:

> Anyone who has set aside the law of Moses dies without mercy on the evidence of two or three witnesses. How much worse punishment, do you think, will be deserved by the one who has trampled underfoot the Son of God, and has profaned the blood of the covenant by which he was sanctified, and has outraged the Spirit of grace? (10.28–29)

This picture is especially clear in the prophets, where God's messengers relay to the people God's reaction to their constant rejection of Him and His blessings to turn to idolatry.

Hosea 1–3 depicts the relationship between God and His idolatrous people as that of a forlorn lover whose wife is a prostitute. Hosea is instructed to live out what God goes through with His people: Hosea marrys a prostitute and when she repeatedly cheats on him, he repeatedly takes her back.

Jeremiah describes idolatrous Judah as a donkey in heat whose lust cannot be restrained and who is so quick to sin that "none who seek her need weary themselves," and, "You have played the whore with many lovers; ...Where have you not been ravished? By the waysides you have sat awaiting lovers. ...You have polluted the land with your vile whoredom" (2.23–24; 3.1–2). This is more graphic language that we are used to reading in the Bible as God unambiguously describes how He sees sin. As shocking as this language might be to some, Ezekiel uses even stronger language to depict the insult that sin is to God (esp. ch 23).

This—not the sanitized, sugar-coated version of sin that we may think of—is the picture that we must see. This is the true nature of sin and seeing it will lead to a heart that is distressed over the things we see and hear, even as God's heart is distressed over it.

Sin is an affront to God's glory. Romans 3.23 is a familiar passage, but it is easy to miss the significance: when we sin, we fall short of *God's glory.* Sin is not merely the breaking of an arbitrary set of rules. Although there is an aspect of rule-breaking in sin (cf. 1 John 3.4), it is much more than that. God's laws are derived from God's character and God's glory. To sin is not to fall short of random commands, but to fall short of the very glory of God.

Sin is opposed to our calling. We are called to something far better than sin. God has plans for our lives that are far greater than turning back to the very things from which He has called us. The thought of doing so is counterintuitive. Returning to that way of life is, as Peter describes it, like a dog returning to its vomit (2 Pet 2.20–22). From the human perspective, it's opposed to common sense. From the spiritual view, it's opposed to what we are called to.

We will spend the next two chapters talking about our high and noble calling and come back in the final three chapters to talk about passages like 2 Timothy 1.8–9 and 2 Peter 1.3–4 in more detail. For now, it is sufficient to say that we are called to a holy calling and to be partakers of the divine nature; sin is trying to undo all of that.

Two of the scariest words in the English language are "malignant cancer." It can kill in months or drag out over torturous years. Sometimes the cure seems almost as bad as the disease and sometimes, even when cured, the disease comes back again and again. It can bring a person to its mercy and often there is nothing that we can do but stand by and watch helplessly. But cancer doesn't hold a candle to what sin does to our souls—and that's the understatement of the year.

We must see sin for what it is if we are ever going to be the holy people God wants us to be.

Holiness

With this framework in place, we can now turn our attention to our call to holiness. In 1 Peter 1, Peter speaks of holiness in two basic ways: how to be holy and why to be holy.

> Therefore, preparing your minds for action, and being sober-minded, set your hope fully on the grace that will be brought to you at the revelation of Jesus Christ. As obedient children, do not be conformed to the passions of your former ignorance, but as he who called you is holy, you also be holy in all your conduct, since it is written, "You shall be holy, for I am holy." And if you call on him as Father who judges impartially according to each one's deeds, conduct yourselves with fear throughout the time of your exile, knowing that you were ransomed from the futile ways inherited from your forefathers, not with perishable things such as silver or gold, but with the precious blood of Christ, like that of a lamb without blemish or spot. (1 Pet 1.13–19)

How to be holy. Peter's teaching on how to be holy can be summed up quite simply: mental preparation. "Girding up the loins of your mind" is, quite literally, the instruction he gives. "Girding up the loins" refers to the gathering and tucking away of garments to prepare for action and thus became idiomatic for any sort of preparation, mental preparation in this case.

Clearly, then, holiness is something that will take effort on our part. God is not going to come down and whack us with the Holy Stick and, just like that, make us holy and solve our sin problem. Holiness begins by us preparing our minds for holiness.

Peter speaks of three different aspects of mental preparation. First, Peter says *to be sober-minded.* In context, Peter's point is not limited to drug- or alcohol-related inebriation, but a broader sort of mental sobriety. To prepare the mind for holiness, we must rid ourselves of whatever might prevent such focus. We must keep our minds clear of distractions that would keep us from holiness: greed or envy, pride or lust, deceit or maliciousness, anything that is opposed to what should be the focus of our thoughts. The opposite of what Paul speaks of in Philippians 4.8 are the things to rid from our minds; instead, fill them with those things that are true, honorable, just, pure, and the like. This is how we prepare our minds for action.

Second, Peter says *to set our hope firmly on God's grace* that is brought at the revelation of Christ. This implies, among other things, having a focus that is set on heaven. Look to God. Make a decision. Have a clear path. Have a clear goal. Have a focus on things that are holy, righteous, and spiritual. It's not too different from James exhortation to "establish your hearts" (5.8). The idea of setting your hope on God's grace is being firmly rooted, being strongly established, having a goal and focusing on it above everything else.

The double-emphasis of clearing the mind and focusing on the goal is reminiscent of Hebrews 12.1–2:

Therefore, since we are surrounded by so great a cloud of witnesses, let us also lay aside every weight, and sin which clings so closely, and let us run with endurance the race that is set before us, looking to Jesus, the founder and perfecter of our faith, who for the joy that was set before him endured the cross, despising the shame, and is seated at the right hand of the throne of God.

Several years ago, I heard the story of two competitive brothers. Since the younger, smaller one usually came up on the losing end of the competition, he devised what he thought was a fool-proof way of beating his older brother. They would race, but the race would be about precision, not speed: the one who ran the straightest line would be the winner. So they lined up side by side and picked a tree as the finish line. Off through the snow, the elder brother ran to the tree. The younger one was more methodical and meticulous. He looked straight down and put one foot after the other, careful to line them up, only occasionally looking up to make sure he was headed toward the tree. When the younger brother finally reached the tree and looked back, he was shocked to find that his line weaved back and forth and his brother's steps were straight.

The difference in the two is simple: the one who kept his eyes on the goal ran in a line straigh toward it. The one who was distracted by other things—even something as seemingly worthy as making sure each foot was properly placed—lost focus on the goal and weaved aimlessly back and forth. He had no clue where he was going in relation to his goal.

So also it is with our walk as Christians. When we set our hope firmly on Christ and on God's grace, when we look to the joy that is set before us as Christ did, we prepare our minds to be holy.

Third, Peter says, *"as obedient children."* Holiness is, on a fundamental level, found in obedience to God—not according to former lusts, but in submission to God's will. Holiness includes repentance. In other words, we put to death the old man, renew the mind, and put on a new man (Eph 4.22–24; cf. Rom 12.1–2). This renewed mind that leads to obedience is to be all-pervasive: "in all your conduct" (v 15).

Why to be holy. Peter does not stop with the command to be holy; he gives reasons for this call, both implicit and explicit.

Since it is written. It is impossible to overstate the value and power of Scripture, and this is where Peter begins: it is written. The nature of Scripture is made powerfully plain in 2 Timothy 3.16–17, which speaks of its inspired nature, its value in teaching, reproving, correcting, and instructing. Paul concludes this passage by saying Scripture makes the man of God *complete*, equipped for *every* good work. There is nothing that we need to know or do or be that is not revealed in Scripture. No other writing or teaching can make us complete-er and there is no every-er good work for which we need to be equipped. Why should we be holy? Because God said so. And that's enough.

"For I am holy." Peter goes on to quote what is written, God's command to be holy. He is our God and He is holy. In Leviticus, God is not commanding holiness for the sake of giving a command, but holiness as He is holy. Holiness is the main theme of the Levitical laws; the laws' purpose was to make the Israelites the holy people God wanted them to be. Likewise, our goal as Christians is to grow to be more like God; we should look like our Father. Why should we be holy? Because God is holy and He's said for us to be as well. That's more than enough.

God is a righteous judge. Peter is not done yet. He reminds us of a recurring theme of the Bible: judgment according to our deeds. Because judgment will be so, our deeds need to be holy. The point here (and in other passages) is not to make light of God's grace, mercy, and love or to suggest that somehow we can earn our salvation by the amassing of good deeds. Rather, it is a reminder that our response to God's grace, mercy, and love matters: it must be obedient holiness. It is the servant's duty to obey (Luke 17.7–10). Why should we be holy? Because we will be judged according to what we do.

What more could possibly be said to motivate us to holiness? God's word says that we should be holy; God's character holy; God will judge us based on whether we live holy lives or not. But the final aspect of our motivation may be the strongest of all.

Purchased by the blood of Christ. Finally, Peter reminds us that what God has done to save us from ourselves has nothing to do with worthless garbage—Peter's characterization of silver and gold. This is another reminder of how different our outlook should be. Peter cites the things that people find most valuable of all and speaks of it as things to throw in the trash. Instead, we are purchased with the blood of Christ.

Here we are reminded of what Christ endured for us: sweat, work, hurt, sickness, temptation, fear and sadness, rejection and betrayal, death—for *my* sin. And we also find a reminder of what He left behind in order to do so. Not only did He endure these things, but He endured them after leaving heaven.

What do you think He felt when He looked around the world and saw the sin and rejection of God? You think Lot's soul was tortured by what he saw? The crucifixion may be most obvious, but it is not the only suffering Christ endured for us. And He is the one whom we trample underfoot and whose blood we count as common when we choose a life of sin instead of a life of obedient holiness.

Why should we be holy? Because the holy, sinless son of God gave His life to offer us the hope of an inheritance that is imperishable, undefiled, and unfading. If we see the cross clearly, if we understand Jesus' sacrifice as much as is humanly possible, how can we do anything else but be the person God wants us to be?

THE CALL

Self-Denial

Why is it that we sin? Why do we fail to overcome temptation and are not the holy people we are called to be? The answer is simple: too much self. Every sin is, in some way, a manifestation of selfishness. We do what *we* want, rather than what God wants. Whether driven by lust or pride, each sin we commit is a conscious decision to put ourselves and our desires ahead of God's law.

My biggest enemy is me.

In particular, the problem is too much of a fleshly self that causes us to ignore the great promises of God's glory for stupid, temporary, worthless sin. Lewis is absolutely right:

> Indeed, if we consider the unblushing promises of reward and the staggering nature of the rewards promised in the Gospels, it would seem that Our Lord finds our desires not too strong, but too weak. We are half-hearted creatures, fooling about with drink and sex and ambition when infinite joy is offered us, like an ignorant child who wants to go on making mud pies in a slum because he cannot imagine what is meant by the offer of a holiday at the sea. We are far too easily pleased.[1]

This is the essence of sin: ignoring the promises of God because we are too wrapped up in self. The solution to this problem, and ultimately to the problem of sin, is a fundamental principle of Christianity: self-denial.

Deny Self

Just how fundamental is self-denial to Christianity? In Jesus' call for disciples, recorded in three of the four gospels, it is the first requirement:

> Then Jesus told his disciples, "If anyone would come after me, let him deny himself and take up his cross and follow me. For whoever would save his life will lose it, but whoever loses his life for my sake will find it. For what will it profit a man if he gains the whole world and forfeits his soul? Or what shall a man give in return for his soul? For the Son of Man is going to come with his angels in the glory of his Father, and then he will repay each person according to what he has done." (Matt 16.24–27)

This is, to some degree, a bewildering demand. It's not a call to some mild form of asceticism, like a diet where we temporary give up a few things we like; nor is it a call to be merely a "weekend warrior" for Christ where we turn our lives and our focus and our thoughts to God once a week. Jesus says that we must completely deny ourselves. We must renounce our right to life—all life, not just a few hours on Sunday. Our desires, hopes, aims, ambitions, plans, and goals all must be put to death for His sake. Barclay says,

> To deny oneself means in every moment of life to say no to self and yes to God. To deny oneself means once, finally and for all to dethrone self and to enthrone God. To deny oneself means to obliterate self as the dominant principle of life, and to make God the ruling principle, more, the ruling passion of life.[2]

The American cult of selfishness—my rights, my way, my freedom to choose, my entitlements, my self-fulfillment, my self-actualization—is utterly foreign to the Christianity that Jesus established. He calls for the death of self, and our selfish entitlements cannot stand up against such a call.

Many sins committed in our culture are rooted in entitlement and self-indulgence. "I want to be happy on my terms," we say. "I have that right." "How dare someone else tell me what to do!" This attitude works perfectly well in the United States of America where denial of God is growing more prevalent every day. But it will not work in the Kingdom of Heaven where denial of self is the standard to which all would-be disciples are held.

In fact, our culture's "liberating" views are really more infantile than they are enlightened:

> A baby will cover his face with a blanket and think no one can see him. He has not yet learned that there is any other perspective than his own. He thinks if he cannot see you, then you cannot see him. That seems to be how many adults live their lives as well. The only things that matter to them are what *they* are going through, and how it affects *them*. The self-centeredness of an infant has grown into the selfishness of an adult.[3]

Some ask what the harm of private sins are. After all, "this sin doesn't hurt anyone else," they claim. "God wants me to be happy," others say. Of course He does! The problem isn't that this perspective is false (as is sometimes alleged), but rather that we think our fleshly desires are a sufficient barometer to measure the kind of happines God wants for us. Simply stated, God doesn't want us to be happy so much as He wants us to be crucified. The one who clings to personal rights is not following Jesus; private sins matter because they are rooted in self-indulgence. What Jesus asks first of all is to deny self; a life that is rooted in self is not a life that follows Him.

Immediately after the call to deny self is the demand to take a cross and follow Jesus. Within the context of the gospel story, this requirement follows immediately upon Peter's confession of Jesus as Christ and rejection of Jesus as a *suffering* Christ (Matt 16.13–23). The demand to take a cross explains why it is so vital that Peter—and modern disciples as well—must come to terms with the sort of Messiah Jesus was; otherwise, we have no hope of grasping the sort of disciple we need to be. The so-called "health and wealth gospel" falls on its face at this point, as does anything else we are tempted to turn the gospel into. Anything less than a crucified Christ and crucified disciples is not the gospel of Jesus and is false Christianity.

Taking up a cross does not necessarily mean a *literal* one (though for the early disciples it often did), but it is very much a *real* cross that we are called to carry. To the original audience, the meaning would have been clear: when a man from one of their villages took up a cross and went off with a little band of Roman soldiers, he was on a one-way journey; he would not be coming back. They would have readily understood: taking up the cross meant the utmost in self-denial.[4] It is not bearing up under a difficulty or facing an adversity; it is deliberately dying to self.

In Luke, the taking up of a cross is *daily* (9.23). The call is a constant call to self-denial. It is not just great moments of sacrifice to which we are called to muster up our strength to do something profound for Jesus, but every day that we are called to be sacrificial. We must always deny self.

Martyrdom, a literal cross, may be in store for some, but is not the case for most. Yet the cross is for all. The call is sacrifice of self in daily life. It is not, then, something that can be completed, but a lifelong task.

For those seeking motivation, Jesus gives that as well with three consecutive "for" clauses (Matt 16.25–27). First, trying to preserve one's life will result in the loss of it. Second, following this path makes no sense. Third, Jesus will judge based on our actions. As with other judgment passages, we find a strong indication that we cannot live selfish lives and be pleasing to Him.

Crucify Self

Paul says, "I have been crucified with Christ. It is no longer I who live, but Christ who lives in me. And the life I now live in the flesh I live by faith in the Son of God, who loved me and gave himself for me" (Gal 2.20).

We will come back to this passage later, so I'll just make one brief point here. The context has to do with dying to the law and being set free from its burden. Even so, the larger biblical context suggests additional meaning beyond just the law. Longenecker suggests that it is not only death to the jurisdiction of the law, but also death to the jurisdiction of one's own ego. In this context, the "I" is the flesh—any of those things antagonistic to the Spirit.[5] Instead of the jurisdiction of self, the jurisdiction of Christ now rules the believer's life.

This call is, then, the same call to take up a cross daily. This, again, is the requirement for every Christian. It is what we are to do. It is who we are to be: a people who have crucified self.

The denial of self is patterned after a crucified Christ and is the message of a crucified Christ. It is, as Paul says, foolishness in the eyes of the world and will never be anything but that (cf. 1 Cor 1.18ff). Even so, we cannot afford to water down this most stringent call to self-denial.

Sacrifice Self

In addition to self-denial by a crucified life, Paul also speaks of self-sacrifice:

> I appeal to you therefore, brothers, by the mercies of God, to present your bodies as a living sacrifice, holy and acceptable to God, which is your spiritual worship. Do not be conformed to this world, but be transformed by the renewal of your mind, that by testing you may discern what is the will of God, what is good and acceptable and perfect. (Rom 12.1–2)

Christian worship is self-sacrificial worship of our bodies. Real worship is offering our whole selves to God. We are called to give ourselves totally to God, and He will accept no less. Worship is thus tied to behavior, which is just another way of talking about self-denial: those who have presented their bodies as a sacrifice no longer belong to themselves but to God. We no longer have say over our behavior. We are God's property. We have given ourselves to Him and must behave according to His law. God doesn't want something *from* us; he wants *us*.[6] The call is, again, denying self and enthroning God, committing to obey Him rather than responding to every urge of self.

That we are called to be *living* sacrifices emphasizes the ongoing nature of the sacrifice, like the daily taking up of the cross. The sacrifices that Jews and pagans knew and participated in were once-for-all killings. They took their animal to the temple, killed it, and the sacrifice was complete. Even Christ's sacrifice on the cross was a one-time event. Our sacrifice is a living one, a constant dedication to God—constant self-denial.

The sacrifice we make of self is also to be holy, even as we saw in the last chapter. Holiness conveys the idea of something or someone being consecrated or dedicated, set apart for God, and given over entirely to Him. The whole self, then, is constantly and totally given to God and so our behavior is set apart to Him. The believer is to be God's and God's alone. The body, this living sacrifice, is every day given to Him and constantly dedicated to Him.

It could be easy to read verse 1 and walk away thinking that, as long as we control our bodies, our minds are free to roam as they please. This conclusion opposes a large section of Jesus' teaching in the Sermon on the Mount. In the immediate context, one would need to forego Romans 12.2, which calls for a renewal of the mind. It is not only the body and actions that matter, but the mind as well. As Christians, we can no longer think like unbelievers do. We can no longer think selfishly. We can no longer think as we once thought. In this self-sacrifice, we must be transformed to think like God: selflessly.

Die to Self

Paul clearly understood Jesus' call to self-denial. In addition to his discussion of self-crucifixion and self-sacrifice, Paul speaks of the implications of baptism and death to self:

> What shall we say then? Are we to continue in sin that grace may abound? By no means! How can we who died to sin still live in it? Do you not know that all of us who have been baptized into Christ Jesus were baptized into his death? We were buried therefore with

him by baptism into death, in order that, just as Christ was raised from the dead by the glory of the Father, we too might walk in newness of life.

For if we have been united with him in a death like his, we shall certainly be united with him in a resurrection like his. We know that our old self was crucified with him in order that the body of sin might be brought to nothing, so that we would no longer be enslaved to sin. For one who has died has been set free from sin. Now if we have died with Christ, we believe that we will also live with him. We know that Christ, being raised from the dead, will never die again; death no longer has dominion over him. For the death he died he died to sin, once for all, but the life he lives he lives to God. So you also must consider yourselves dead to sin and alive to God in Christ Jesus.

Let not sin therefore reign in your mortal body, to make you obey its passions. Do not present your members to sin as instruments for unrighteousness, but present yourselves to God as those who have been brought from death to life, and your members to God as instruments for righteousness. For sin will have no dominion over you, since you are not under law but under grace. (Rom 6.1–14)

We do not have the time or space for a full investigation of the text, but some brief comment can be made here about how thorough a call is made for overcoming temptation and self-denial.[7]

Shall we continue in sin? This rhetorical question fundamentally challenges us to a changed and selfless life. It is not a natural thing to do if we are following after self. Continuing in sin, after all, is what the old man *wants to do* (cf. Rom 3.23; 7.15–20). That we would continue in sin carries the idea of remaining in it, being in continued bondage to sin, staying where we are because we like it, refusing to budge from habitual sin. Paul will have none of it because Christ will have none of it! This is not the life we are called to live. Self-indulgence is not the life of the Christian.

How can we who died to sin still live in it? With our self-denial and self-sacrifice comes the repudiation of sin. Acquiescence to sin is incompatible with Christianity. We cannot live that way if we have died to self. To have died to sin is to be utterly out of any relation to it.

We too might walk in newness of life. Having gone through the transformation symbolized by baptism—death to self, burial of self with Christ, new life in Him—we should walk in newness of life. The life of sin and self-indulgence that we lived before is not the life that we live now. We will discuss this more in the next chapter.

Our old self was crucified with him. The "old self" is a phrase Paul uses two other times (Eph 4; Col 3), and each time he uses it he does so with a verb of repudiation. The old self is to be crucified, that is, utterly destroyed. Sin is no longer supreme; the power of sin is broken in the believer. This is not to say that the believer will never again sin, but that sin must be the exception rather than the rule. Previously, when in bondage to sin and self, purity was unnatural; now, sin is.

In order that the body of sin might be brought to nothing. Here is the purpose of this self-crucifixion: freeing us from our own sinful inclinations; freeing us from bondage to sin; freeing us from *self.* Our terrible condition changes because of our participation in Christ's death. In what way is it changed?

So that we should no longer be enslaved to sin. If slavery to sin is no longer the case, then we previously *were* enslaved to sin. A life of self-pursuit is a life of slavery. The so-called liberation the world offers is nothing more than bondage to sin. Coming to Christ and sacrificing self frees us from the domination of sin.

For one who has died has been set free from sin. As long as a slave is alive, he is under the rule of his master, but when a slave dies his master no longer has claim over him. We were enslaved to sin because that is where the old self would lead us. When we died with Christ, buried the old self, and were raised to a new life in Him, sin had no more claim on us. Since we have been freed, we must live a life that is set free from sin.

So you must consider yourselves dead to sin and alive to God in Christ Jesus. Christ died to sin and the Christian died with Him in baptism; so the believer is dead to sin as well and should recognize that fact. The Christian must realize that he is dead to sin, a truth that negates the notion that sin is an inevitable part of our daily lives and that "we all sin all the time." No! We are dead to sin!

The Christian is not immunized against temptation or there would be no need for so many warnings and exhortations to remain pure and live the new life. There are still temptations and there is still sin, but the situation is completely different. The unbeliever sins because he is enslaved to sin; we sinned because we were in slavery. But we have been freed. The sin of the Christian is out of character. He has been delivered from the dominion of sin. As such, we must strive to live in this way.

Let not sin therefore reign in your mortal body, to make you obey its passions. Here again is the presumption that sin and temptation linger. The Christian is not promised a life where temptation is blissfully excluded. Sin is still an active force, but it is no longer supreme. When we died to self, we were set free by Christ. We cannot continue to live like a slave when Christ has set us free.

Do not present your members to sin as instruments for unrighteousness. Here is a life of slavery to sin, willingly giving ourselves to sin to do whatever it tells us—a life of self-indulgence, a life where we go after what we want and what we think will bring happiness and fulfillment rather than what God tells us to do.

Present yourselves to God…and your members to God as instruments for righteousness. Self and sin are dead. Instead of giving ourselves back to the terrible slave-driver of sin, we must give ourselves to the one who freed us from it, the one who gave us the opportunity to put the old self to death so we can walk in a new life. Since the Christian belongs to God, his body is to be used for God's righteous purposes.

Sin will have no dominion over you. One last reminder: the life of a Christian is a life where sin is no longer master, because self is no longer master.

Christianity—and with it, defeating sin—is all about getting rid of self: self-denial, self-crucifixion, self-sacrifice, death to self. If we try to cling to our desires, our rights, and our entitlements, then we will constantly live a life of sin.

We often talk about Christianity as a selfless religion, though usually from the perspective of humility and service. That is a good and proper point of emphasis, but selflessness must not end there. Self-denial must be pervasive in every aspect of our lives as we put to death our desires, our pride, our ambitions, and everything else about us, replacing self with Christ's rule in our hearts.

This makes no sense to the world around us. Nor should it; it is patterned after a crucified Christ. There were no human witnesses of Calvary who saw Jesus' death as victory. The Messianic hope was glory and liberation; instead, the Messiah was humiliated and killed. Yet, in spite of our human perspective, it *was* victory.

Likewise, there is no one who would look at the self-denial a Christian is called to and call it wisdom or a good path to achieving what is best for us. It is, however, clearly the Christian path because it is the path that our Savior trod. Even as Christ died to overcome sin, so we must also die if we hope to overcome sin and put on a new life.

3

THE CALL

New Life

The previous chapter ended with a brief exposition of Romans 6.1–14, describing in some detail the implications of death to self in relation to sin. Included in that picture is the liberation from sin we receive in the new life. We are called to new life, and this high calling is why it is so vital that we overcome temptation.

Beyond that general principle, what does the new life look like? We find a clear picture of the new life in Colossians 3.1–17.[1]

If then you have been raised with Christ, seek the things that are above, where Christ is, seated at the right hand of God. Set your minds on things that are above, not on things that are on earth. For you have died, and your life is hidden with Christ in God. When Christ who is your life appears, then you also will appear with him in glory.

Put to death therefore what is earthly in you: sexual immorality, impurity, passion, evil desire, and covetousness, which is idolatry. On account of these the wrath of God is coming. In these you too once walked, when you were living in them. But now you must put them all away: anger, wrath, malice, slander, and obscene talk from your mouth. Do not lie to one another, seeing that you have put off the old self with its practices and have put on the new self, which is being renewed in knowledge after the image of its creator. Here there is not Greek and Jew, circumcised and uncircumcised, barbarian, Scythian, slave, free; but Christ is all, and in all.

Put on then, as God's chosen ones, holy and beloved, compassionate hearts, kindness, humility, meekness, and patience, bearing with one another and, if one has a complaint against another, forgiving each other; as the Lord has forgiven you, so you also must forgive. And above all these put on love, which binds everything together in perfect harmony. And let the peace of Christ rule in your hearts, to which indeed you were called in one body. And be thankful. Let the word of Christ dwell in you richly, teaching and admonishing one another in all wisdom, singing psalms and hymns and spiritual songs, with thankfulness in your hearts to God. And whatever you do, in word or deed, do everything in the name of the Lord Jesus, giving thanks to God the Father through him.

The Risen Life (vv 1–4)

One cannot rise from baptism the same person he was when he went into the water. There must be a difference; the one who was baptized has died (cf. Col 2.12; 3.3). Fundamentally, the difference lies in the fact that the Christian's thoughts must be set on the things that are above.

Paul is not demanding a monastic lifestyle of withdrawal from all the work and activities of this world in favor of constant contemplation of eternity. After all, my biggest enemy is *me*, and withdrawing myself into a cave somewhere will not solve the problems of my heart. Rather, everything is to be viewed through the lens of eternity. We are no longer to live as if this world were all that mattered. He will see things, not as they appear to people, but as they appear to God. His standard of values will be God's standard, not the standard of men.

The new life is characterized by ambitions that are not earth-bound and set on transient and inferior objects. We must not look at life from the standpoint of these lower planes. Rather, we must look at everything from Christ's exalted standpoint and judge everything by the standards of the new creation to which we now belong, not by those of the old order to which we have said a final farewell.

Christ is here described as "your life," which is no surprise to anyone who is familiar with Paul's writings (cf. Gal 2.20; Phil 1.21). And we understand the basic concept when this terminology is used in the world around us. To say that "music is my life" or "I live for sports" suggests that meaning and fulfillment is found in those things. For the Christian, Christ is his life. Jesus dominates his thought, fills his life, and gives it meaning. This is why the Christian sets his mind and heart on the things which are above, not the things of the world. He judges everything by the light of the cross. In this light, the world's ambitions, activities, and wealth are seen in their true value. The Christian is delivered from the earthly things and enabled to set his whole heart on the things which are above.

The Garments of the Grave (vv 5–11)

The imagery that stands behind the exhortation is that of changing garments. In verse 8, the word translated "put them all away" is the regular Greek word for putting off clothes. The next section begins with what is to be "put on" in its place (v 12).

The things to be put off are exactly what we talked about in the last chapter: self-centeredness and all private desires and ambitions. Self must have no place in the our lives. We must put to death every part of self and personality which is against God.

Fleshly Sins. Paul begins with what can be described as sins of the flesh.

Fornication and Uncleanness. Purity, as taught by Christians, was a new virtue to the pagan world—much as it is today. In Hellenistic culture, relationships before marriage and outside marriage brought no shame and were the normal practice. They, as modern culture does, regarded the sexual appetite as a thing to be gratified, not controlled.

Passion and Desire. People who have not been liberated from the bondage of sin by death to self are slaves to their passions, driven by desire for the wrong things. Those so enslaved have no idea how to control various desires and never even attempt to do so.

Covetousness. Covetousness is an insatiable desire for something, usually at the expense of someone else. It is like trying to fill with water a bowl with a hole in it. The materialistic side of covetousness sees happiness as always being just over the horizon of the next purchase.

Covetousness covers a wide range of sin, each of which begins with unbridled desire for something: desire for money, which leads to theft; desire for honor, which leads to evil ambition; desire for power, which leads to sadistic tyranny; desire for someone (which, given the context, may be the best fit in Colossians 3), which leads to sexual sin.

Covetousness is equated with idolatry and rightfully so. The covetous person's whole life is dominated by the desire to get money, honor, power, people, or any number of other things. A life so dominated is a life devoid of God; He has been replaced with lesser desires.

Sins of the Mouth and Heart. From the flesh, Paul turns to the heart and specifically the mouth, the well from which issues of the heart proceed. A right heart is fundamental to a right life, and that may be implied here as well. However, the emphasis in this text is on the verbal expression of these emotions.

Anger, Wrath, and Malice. Anger and wrath may be essentially synonymous and serve a rhetorical function of emphasizing all sorts of evil thinking. If the two are to be distinguished, wrath is the sudden blaze which is quickly kindled and quickly dies; anger is the long-lasting, slow-burning emotion which refuses to be pacified. Both are contrary to the Christian life.

Obviously, there is a place for the righteous indignation that God and Jesus each exemplify in Scripture, and Paul speaks of an anger that is not sinful (Eph 4.26). The anger and wrath of Colossians 3 is clearly the pervasive emotions of the old man; the new man's anger is not of this sort.

Malice is an all-pervading evil, viciousness of the mind from which various individual vices spring. Paul's purpose is probably not to single out these specific sins, but to use the three words together to express the attitude of anger and ill will toward others that so often leads to hasty and nasty speech.[2]

Slander, Foul Talk, and Lying. Again, this sort of speech is characteristic of the old life; the new life cannot exhibit any of these traits. Christian talk must be kind. Christian talk must be pure. Christian talk must be true.

Divisiveness and Social Prejudices. There is a complete change when one becomes a Christian. The new man cannot look at the world the way he once did. Christianity leads to unity and should liberate us from social prejudices.

The world was divided in ancient times. The Greeks looked down on the barbarians. The Jews looked down on all non-Jews. Everyone looked down on the Scythian (the lowest of the barbarians). The slave was not even classified as a human being, just a living tool.

Christianity destroys and removes all of that divisiveness. It destroys the barriers that come from birth and nationality. It destroys the barriers that come from ritual. It destroys the barriers between the cultured and the uncultured. It destroys the barriers between classes. The new life unites people in Christ.

The Garments of Grace (vv 12–17)

Taking off the garments of the old man is not sufficient. Throughout Scripture, the call is to remove one thing and replace it with another. In these verses, Paul lists virtues to put on.

Paul begins by appealing to the Colossians as "chosen ones, holy and beloved." He is immediately applying the principles of non-divisiveness. These were all words that Jews thought of as belonging to themselves, since they were "holy to the LORD your God … chosen to be a people for his treasured possession, out of all the peoples who are on the face of the earth … because the LORD loves you" (Deut 7.6–8). But Paul takes these terms and applies them to the Gentiles. All who come to God in Christ are now God's chosen ones, holy, and beloved. As God's new creation whom He has set apart for Himself, Christians should exhibit something of His character.

Virtues to Put On. Notice that all of the virtues listed have to do with personal relationships. There is no mention of things like efficiency, cleverness, diligence, or industry. That is not because these things have no value but because the virtues of Christianity are the things that govern relationships. Christianity is about community. A godly life begins with God ("Love the Lord your God with all your heart…") and turns immediately to others ("...and love your neighbor as yourself"). The new life of holiness is not something that is impractical, theoretical, or merely theological.

Compassion. Compassion is having a heart of pity. Mercy and compassion were not terribly prevalent in the ancient world. Treatment of the widow, the orphan, the aged, and the simple was not with love or for their own good.

The new life is characterized by compassion *because God is compassionate.* The word is derived from a verb which is repeatedly used of Jesus' compassionate reaction to people in need (e.g., Mark 6.34). The noun is used of "the *mercies* of God" (Rom 12.1) and describes God as "the father of *mercies*" (2 Cor 1.3).

Kindness. According to Barclay, ancient writers defined the Greek word as the virtue of the man whose neighbor's good is as dear to him as his own. It is, in essence, the practice of loving one's neighbor as himself. Kindness can, however, be stern or demanding when needed; the word is used of Jesus' yoke being *easy.*

The new life is characterized by kindness *because God is kind.* "Taste and see that the LORD is *good,*" David says (Psa 34.8). God's "kindness and severity" are displayed in His dealings with men (Rom 11.22), and His kindness is designed to bring mankind to repentance (Rom 2.4). The call of the Christian is to be like the Father, which Jesus implies when He calls His hearers to love their enemies; in so doing, "You will be sons of the Most High, for he is kind to the ungrateful and the evil" (Luke 6.35).

Humility. Christian humility is based on the awareness that we are created, an acknowledgment that governs our relationship with God. He is creator; we are creature. What else can we feel in His presence but humility?

Christian humility is also based on the belief that all mankind is God's creation, a realization that governs our relationship with our fellow man. No matter how different or how irritating he may be, all others are also created in God's image. There is no room for arrogance when we are all royal lineage. There is stark difference between this mindset and that of the old man. Consider society at large, filled with tensions that spring from pride and self-assertiveness. Humility has always been the call of God's people. The one who would walk with God must be the one willing to humble himself (e.g., Mic 6.8). God chooses to dwell with those who are of a humble and contrite spirit (Isa 57.15)

The new life is characterized by humility *because Christ is humble.* He willingly left heaven behind to put on flesh and endure the cross. He lowered Himself to the position of the lowest servant in the household to wash the feet of the disciples. He loved by giving Himself for our good.

Meekness. Meekness is closely related to gentleness, but it is not merely a natural, gentle disposition that some have. Aristotle characterized it as the happy mean between too much anger and too little anger; it is always being angry at the right time and never being angry at the wrong time. Meekness is the control of strength—having the ability to run roughshod over others and choosing not to do so.

The new life is characterized by meekness *because Christ is meek.* Paul appealed to the Corinthians by the meekness of Christ (2 Cor 10.1), and Jesus' own self-declaration was that He was meek and lowly in heart (Matt 11.29).

Patience. The foolishness of our fellow man does not drive us to cynicism or despair. The insults of our fellow man do not drive us to bitterness and wrath.

The new life is characterized by patience *because God is patient.* The patience of God is included in the revelation of the divine nature along with His compassion and mercy (Exod 34.6). God is patient toward His chosen people (Luke 18.7) and toward the impenitent (Rom 2.4). It is His patience that postpones the day of retribution (Rom 9.22).

Forbearing and Forgiving Spirit. Because he is a forgiven man, the Christian exhibits a forgiving spirit. The penitence of the sinner and his willingness to forgive others go hand in hand. One of the chief evidences of true penitence is a forgiving spirit. When our eyes have been opened to the enormity of our sin against God, the injuries which others cause us appear, by comparison, to be insignificant. If, however, we have an exaggerated view of the offenses of others, we have a minimized view of our own sin. Those who fail to forgive others are usually the same as those who find it difficult to confess their own wrongs.

The new life is to be characterized by forgiveness *because God is forgiving.* Again, this is part of the revelation of God's divine character (Exod 34.6) and the refrain of hope for sinners throughout the Old Testament, a point we will return to in chapter 8. The parallel passage in Ephesians 4.32 directly connects our call to forgive with God's nature of forgiveness.

Love. Finally, we are told to put on love. Love is the binding power that holds the whole Christian body together. In Galatians 5.6, love is the active expression of a saving faith. In Galatians 5.22, it is the fundamental fruit of the spirit. In Romans 13.9–10, love sums up all the commandments. In 1 Corinthians 12–13, it is—of all Christian gifts—the supreme one. On the lips of Jesus it is the greatest and second commandment on which all of the Law and prophets depend. It is absolutely impossible to overstate the value and necessity of love.

The new life is to be characterized by love *because God is love* and has shown love beyond our comprehension (1 John 4.7–10).

Singing. It may be a surprise that Paul turns next to singing. Sadly, the typical practice among many churches is to extricate this verse to argue the *how* of singing rather than letting its context show us that the point is *why.* Paul argues that singing is first an expression of thankfulness for this new life and the peace of Christ which comes with it. Second, it is a way of teaching, edifying, and exhorting.

This latter point is why hymns must be meaningful, not just beautiful. It is why singing must be rooted in the word of Christ dwelling richly in us. Martin well says, "The idea of 'hymns' as teaching vehicles … puts a question mark against much 'free' worship with pitiably weak, sentimental, and introspective chorus/song singing in some churches today."[3]

Do All in the Name of Jesus. To do all, word and deed, in the name of Jesus is to do everything in the reputation and character of Jesus, to do everything with Him in mind. For everything to be governed by the name of Jesus becomes a test of any action. Can we do it while calling upon the name of Jesus? Can we do it asking for His help, His guidance, and His presence?

Likewise, it becomes a test of any word. Can we speak it and in the same breath speak the name of Jesus? Can we speak it remembering that He will hear—and asking Him to hear? If a person brings every word and deed into the presence of Jesus Christ, he will not go wrong:

> The Christian… when confronted by a moral issue, may not find any explicit word of Christ relating to its particular details. But the

question may be asked: 'What is the Christian to do here? Can I do this without compromising my Christian confession? Can I do it... "in the name of the Lord Jesus"—whose reputation is at stake in the conduct of his known followers? And can I thank God the Father through him for the opportunity of doing this thing?' Even then, the right course of action may not be unambiguously clear, but such questions, honestly faced, will commonly provide surer ethical guidance than special regulations may do. It is often easy to get around special regulations; it is less easy to get around so comprehensive a statement of Christian duty as this verse supplies. In the NT and the OT alike it is insisted that our relation to God embraces and controls the whole of life, and not only those occasions which are sometimes described as 'religious' in a narrow sense of the word.[4]

The new life is a God-centered life. It is founded on the old self dying and a new self being raised with Christ. It includes a list of virtues that are wholly rooted in God's character, either displayed in Scripture or through the person of Christ. It is governed by the principle of bringing all life into the presence of Christ.

These three chapters are not an exhaustive discussion of what Christians are called to be, but they should serve as a solid foundation to build on. They answer the *why* of overcoming temptation: we are called to be holy; we are called to deny self; we are called to a new life that is characterized by the very traits of God.

Such a calling is incompatible with sin. But how do we overcome a foe who knows our weaknesses so well and can use a seemingly-limitless supply of temptations to exploit those weaknesses? The next step is to get to know our enemies a little better.

THE ENEMY

Satan

A coach studies film of his opponent for good reason. The hope of winning the game increases as he knows more about the team against whom he will compete; knowledge of the opponent increases the chances of winning. Likewise, there is good reason why generals and presidents are willing to pay a lot of money for intelligence about their enemies in times of war; knowing the enemy is fundamental to success in battle.

This is also true of our battle with temptation. Our chances of winning the battle are increased by knowledge of our enemies. Over the next two chapters, we will consider our two biggest enemies, beginning with Satan.

Who Is Satan?

One of the most frequently asked questions about Satan is his origins. While a full study is outside the scope of this book, it is helpful to consider briefly. It is easy to misconstrue the power of Satan and think of him as being nearly omnipotent and omnipresent. We sometimes think that he always knows what we are thinking, he is everywhere we go, he has unlimited power to get into our lives. But Satan is not God. One of the things explicitly made clear in Scripture is that God is

God alone. However powerful and pervasive Satan may be, he is not God.

As to his origin, the simple answer is that we cannot know for sure; no specifics are given to us. There are, however, implications that provide a safe assumption of his origin. We know that through Christ, God created all things, including the spiritual beings in heaven (Col 1.15–17). We know that everything God created was good, as demanded by His nature (cf. Gen 1.31). He could have created nothing that was inherently evil. It is safe to infer, then, that Satan was a good spiritual being who, through an act of his free will, chose to rebel against God.[1]

Far more significant than understanding his origins is understanding his aim. The word *Satan* is the standard Hebrew word for *adversary* and is used throughout the Old Testament of anyone in an adversarial role—even the Angel of the Lord (Num 22.22). It is clear, however, that there is one adversary who stands especially opposed to God and His people. This is Satan's role throughout the Bible.

In Genesis 3, Satan appears to tempt mankind to rebel against God. In Job 1–2 he accused Job of being righteous for pay and instigates Job's plight. In Zechariah 3.1–2, he accuses Joshua the high priest. In Matthew 4.1–10, he stands against Christ—God in the flesh—and tempts Him. Satan uses people, even people who are well-meaning like Peter, to oppose God (Matt 16.23). Satan schemes against God and His people, going to war with us, attacking with fiery arrows (Eph 6.11–12, 16). He is described as an adversary who is like a roaring lion, seeking to devour its prey (1 Pet 5.8). He is described as an accuser who (before he was cast out) accused the brethren day and night before God (Rev 12.9–10).

The picture is clear: Satan is our adversary. He strives to draw us away from God by deceit. He strives to draw us away from God by suffering. He strives to draw us away from God with well-meaning people who distract us from what is important or tempt us to do what we should not. He strives to draw us away from God by open attack, by accusation, and by warfare. He strives to draw us away from God by creeping up on us stealthily and pouncing when we are least prepared to defend ourselves.

The implication is unmistakable. Satan is not someone to take lightly. It is easy to think of Satan in the cartoonish, comical images that we have seen in popular culture. He is not that at all.

He certainly is not someone to disbelieve. Perhaps the most dangerous thing we can do is not believe in Satan at all. A growing number of people are perfectly happy to believe in God and heaven but do not want to consider the reality of hell and Satan. We cannot be aware of him or watchful for him or prepare ourselves against him if we do not believe that he is out there ready to attack.

How Does Satan Tempt Us?

The best place to look for an idea of how Satan goes about tempting us is the very first temptation.[2] Neither his aim nor his methods have changed in thousands of years.

> Now the serpent was more crafty than any other beast of the field that the Lord God had made. He said to the woman, "Did God actually say, 'You shall not eat of any tree in the garden'?" And the woman said to the serpent, "We may eat of the fruit of the trees in the garden, but God said, 'You shall not eat of the fruit of the tree that is in the midst of the garden, neither shall you touch it, lest you

die.'" But the serpent said to the woman, "You will not surely die. For God knows that when you eat of it your eyes will be opened, and you will be like God, knowing good and evil." So when the woman saw that the tree was good for food, and that it was a delight to the eyes, and that the tree was to be desired to make one wise, she took of its fruit and ate, and she also gave some to her husband who was with her, and he ate. (Gen 3.1–6)

The Attack. First, consider this scene from Satan's perspective. Notice his approach. It is casual and subtle, without any indication of who he is or what he is up to. Satan begins with a simple question that is disarmingly small-talkish and a subtle exaggeration that is pivotal in turning Eve from God.

Although there is plenty of deceit built into his question, Satan does not begin with an open lie. He begins by asking if what he heard was true: can you really not eat anything in the garden? The question does not necessarily set off a warning that he is the deceiver and an enemy.

Consider what the subtle exaggeration in the question would do to Eve's thinking. No, God had not said that. In fact, God had not said anything of the kind. He said the opposite; they could eat whatever they wanted, save the fruit of one tree. But the question and exaggeration emphasize the prohibition. It makes it seem outrageous and a monstrous deprivation that God is trying to keep them from something that they should have access to. Instead of thinking about all of the good things that God has blessed them with, Eve is thinking about the one thing she cannot have.

Although he does not come out and say so, Satan is questioning the very goodness of God and painting Him a miser. Perhaps most significantly, Satan projects the picture of a false rivalry between God and man—that God is man's enemy and man needs to do something about it to rectify the situation. Rather than a gracious, beneficial creator, God is seen as opposing man's best interest.

And what happens when you tell someone that he *can't* have something, and he starts obsessing about that one thing he cannot have? It may be most evident in small children, but emphasizing the prohibition has the same impact on people of all ages: it is what we cannot have that we most want. How quickly we ignore all of the abundant blessings that God has given us as soon as we see the one forbidden thing. That thing suddenly becomes the apple of our eye. It becomes the thing we want most of all, and we want nothing to stand in our way of that.

Notice also the subtlety of Satan's lies. "You will not surely die," he says. In some sense this is true. They did not immediately fall down dead nor were they immediately cast into the eternal death of hell. But clearly it is false: they began to die physically, falling under the certain penalty of death, and they were separated from God in a way they never had been before. "You will become like God," Satan said. Again, in a sense it is true; God admitted as much (v 22). But clearly it is false: they were *already* like God (1.26), and eating the fruit ultimately made them less like God: sinners and subject to death.

The Sin. Next, consider Eve's perspective. Her response happened in three basic stages.

She doubted God's word. Eve distrusts God's promise and God's command. Although the text never comes out and says this explicitly, it must be true because Eve began to consider eating the fruit. If she were fully confident in God's commandment and the consequences, her actions would have been different. Had she not doubted God's word, she never would have even considered it. But once there is doubt of God's truthfulness, the perspective changes.

She is concerned with her perspective. Eve is no longer concerned with God's perspective, as she was at the outset (vv 2–3). Once Satan convinces her to doubt God's word, her perspective becomes, "Hey, that looks pretty good." Suddenly, rather than seeing the situation from God's perspective, she sees it from hers. We have already talked about the need to deny self in Chapter 2 and will talk more about the problem of self in the next chapter, but we see it rearing its ugly head here. When Eve lost focus on God by doubting His word, she immediately replaced concern for God's will with concern for self. When she became concerned with self, she saw the temptation from a fleshly perspective that almost invariably leads to sin. At this point, the battle is nearly lost.

She trusted her assessment. Eve replaces confidence in God's word with confidence in her ability to judge the matter rightly. She examined it from her perspective and decided it would taste good, it was nice to look it, and it would make her a better person—like God! And because she had lost her Godward focus and was concerned with herself, she trusted her own assessment more than God's promise and ate.

This is the picture of all sin, of all temptation. Satan's attacks are always subtle, deceitful, and appealing. His goal is always to distract our focus from God and put it on ourselves. And the most dangerous thing we can ever do is look at temptation and trust our own assessment of it. We must trust God's word. We must trust His promises. We must look at everything through that lens. Through our eyes, it will always look good.

Through our eyes, it will always look appealing. Through the eternal truth of God's word, it will always look bad. It is when we doubt God's word that we set ourselves up to sin.

Why Does He Tempt Us?

Fundamentally, Satan tempts us because he is against God. We have not been told all of the motivating factors for his rebellion, but one thing is clear: he hates God. If we are on God's side, he hates us. We can, however, trace Satan's attack on mankind to something even more specific, particularly as it relates to his fall.[3]

Before Christ came, Satan seems to have had full access to heaven. Throughout the Old Testament, with one exception (1 Chron 21.1), Satan is invariably seen in the very presence of God. In Job 1–2, Satan enters with the Sons of God who present themselves before Him. In Zechariah 3, he stands before God's throne to accuse Joshua. In 1 Kings 22, a lying spirit (*the* lying spirit?) volunteers to go forth from the heavenly court to deceive Ahab. Even in Genesis 3, Satan is very much in the presence of God, as he is in Eden where God is present with Adam and Eve. Throughout the Old Testament, Satan is God's presence.

Satan's enduring presence in heaven fits the picture of a judgment that is issued but an execution that is postponed. After the temptation of Eve, Satan is judged to be defeated, but the execution of that judgment did not come until the time of Christ's death and resurrection (Gen 3.15; cf. Heb 2.14, et al.).

Satan's access to heaven also matches the New Testament teaching. There, the casting out of demons and establishment of the kingdom is linked with Satan, the current strongman, being bound (Matt 12.27–29) and falling from heaven (Luke 10.17–19).

More significantly, Jesus directly links His crucifixion, resurrection, and ascension to the final ousting of Satan: "Now is the judgment of this world; now will the ruler of this world be cast out. And I, when I am lifted up from the earth, will draw all people to myself" (John 12.31–32).

This is also the picture in Revelation 12. Here the birth, life, death, resurrection, and ascension of Christ are depicted in graphic, symbolic terms. Corollary to Christ's life on earth was war in heaven:

> Now war arose in heaven, Michael and his angels fighting against the dragon. And the dragon and his angels fought back, but he was defeated, and there was no longer any place for them in heaven. And the great dragon was thrown down, that ancient serpent, who is called the devil and Satan, the deceiver of the whole world—he was thrown down to the earth, and his angels were thrown down with him. And I heard a loud voice in heaven, saying, "Now the salvation and the power and the kingdom of our God and the authority of his Christ have come, for the accuser of our brothers has been thrown down, who accuses them day and night before our God. And they have conquered him by the blood of the Lamb and by the word of their testimony, for they loved not their lives even unto death." (Rev 12.7–11)

At this point, you may well be thinking, "This is all very interesting, but what does it have to do with why we are tempted?" It has *everything* to do with why we are tempted.

> "Therefore, rejoice, O heavens and you who dwell in them! But woe to you, O earth and sea, for the devil has come down to you in great wrath, because he knows that his time is short!"
>
> And when the dragon saw that he had been thrown down to the earth, he pursued the woman who had given birth to the male child. But the woman was given the two wings of the great eagle

so that she might fly from the serpent into the wilderness, to the place where she is to be nourished for a time, and times, and half a time. The serpent poured water like a river out of his mouth after the woman, to sweep her away with a flood. But the earth came to the help of the woman, and the earth opened its mouth and swallowed the river that the dragon had poured from his mouth. Then the dragon became furious with the woman and went off to make war on the rest of her offspring, on those who keep the commandments of God and hold to the testimony of Jesus. (Rev 12.12–17)

Satan tempts us because he has been thrown down. He wages war against those who are righteous. He wages war against those who keep the commandments of God and hold to the testimony of Jesus.

Before Christ, Satan's judgment was not yet complete. After Christ, he has been fully and finally cast down. Woe to us, for he has come down and his wrath is great. And because he was cast out, Satan is furious and pursues with a special vengeance the people of God.

The thought is frightening. But there is great comfort as well, because victory is certain. When Paul speaks of our spiritual warfare in Ephesians 6, he calls us to draw on the "power," "might," and "strength" of the Lord (v 10). These are the very words that he earlier used of God's power, might, and strength shown in His work of raising Jesus from the dead—the very event that assures the defeat of the enemy (1.19–20). He refers to our enemies as spiritual forces "in the heavenly places" (6.12), but this assures us of their eventual defeat as well, because this is the very realm which Christ reigns (1.20).

We meet the same concept in Revelation 12. Satan attacks not because of his power, but because he is defeated—and he knows it. His time is short. We have battles left to fight, but the war is over. We are on the winning side, and it will not be long until we experience full victory.

That is the confidence we can have as Christians when we face Satan head to head: the enemy has already lost and is desperate. He wants you to go down with him. Don't give him that satisfaction. Take the strength and the power and the might of God, because He is the one who rules in the heavenly places. Put on the armor of God and do battle with Satan. You can win, because he is already defeated.

5

THE ENEMY

Self

Our hope of winning the battle with sin increases as we get to know more about our enemy. In addition to Satan, there is another enemy with whom we need to be acquainted. It is the enemy we know best, but like least to identify as such: ourselves. Next to Satan, my biggest enemy is me. I am the one who chooses to sin and to go against God.

Implications Against Self
The Bible indicates that self is the enemy. Consider the implications against self that span the testaments.

Genesis 3. We spoke in the last chapter about Satan's three-fold method of temptation: to convince us to doubt God's command, to view the situation from our own perspective, and to trust our own judgment.

The common element at every point is *self.* I doubt God's commands when *I* am judging their worthiness. I view the situation from my own perspective when I ask how *I* think this temptation looks. I trust my own judgment when I suppose that *I* know more about it than God. The entire process is rooted in self. Satan's goal is to pit me against God, to create a false rivalry where I feel that God is an enemy withholding something from me, making me want to rebel against Him. Satan's hope is to use me against me.

Perhaps the hardest thing is admitting this to ourselves. The last person we like to blame about anything is ourselves. We see this even in Genesis 3. God arrives and asks questions designed to prompt confession. Instead, "The man said, 'The woman whom you gave to be with me, she gave me fruit of the tree, and I ate.' Then the Lord God said to the woman, 'What is this that you have done?' The woman said, 'The serpent deceived me, and I ate'" (Gen 3.12–13). Our first inclination—things have not changed since this scene—is to point the finger elsewhere. "Well, I'm only human," we say. Or, "I have this weakness." Whatever excuses we may have, they lay the blame elsewhere and refuses to acknowledge that the enemy is self. The sooner we accept responsibility, the sooner we can properly fight the battle.

Wisdom Literature. The wisdom books of the Bible also suggest that the enemy is self and we are culpable. The preacher says, "See, this alone I found, that God made man upright, but they have sought out many schemes" (Ecc 7.29). The problem is not that we were made sinful beings. We were not even made morally neutral. We were created upright. And then mankind universally and deliberately turned from God. We are to blame. We have clouded moral issues. We have refused the straight way. It is our fault, not our fate, that we are sinful people.[1]

Solomon adds, "There is a way that seems right to a man, but its end is the way to death" (Prov 14.12). There is a path that to our thinking seems like a perfectly fine way to go, but if it is not what God has told us is the right way, the rightness of it is a phantom that arises from self-deception. We go astray and judge falsely when we judge without regard to God and His word and follow only our opinions.[2] Our view, our perspective, and our judgment of the right way is not reliable. The result of this sort of judgment is clear as well. The book of Judges ends with a lengthy section bracketed by two statements that "everyone did what was right in his own eyes" (17.6; 21.25). This inclusio[3] frames some of the darkest chapters of the history of Israel—one morally depraved scene after another—and clearly shows the result of following one's own judgment.

Our own judgment will inevitably and invariably lead us astray—just as it did with Eve and the people of Judges 17–21, and just as the wisdom of Proverbs and Ecclesiastes say is the universal truth.

Jesus. The notion that we are most responsible for our sinfulness does not end in the Old Testament. In Mark 7, Jesus' disciples had been criticized for eating with unwashed hands. The Pharisees are all worked up about the tradition of the elders being broken, so Jesus tells them that they are breaking God's laws for their traditions and that their idea of what defiles a person is all wrong:

> And he called the people to him again and said to them, "Hear me, all of you, and understand: There is nothing outside a person that by going into him can defile him, but the things that come out of a person are what defile him." And when he had entered the house and left the people, his disciples asked him about the parable. And he said to them, "Then are you also without understanding? Do you not see that whatever goes into a person from outside cannot defile him, since it enters not his heart but his stomach, and is expelled?" (Thus he declared all foods clean.) And he said, "What comes out of a person is what defiles him. For from within, out of the heart of man, come evil thoughts, sexual immorality, theft,

murder, adultery, coveting, wickedness, deceit, sensuality, envy, slander, pride, foolishness. All these evil things come from within, and they defile a person." (vv 14–23)

That which is from within is what defiles a person. Verse 19 makes it clear that the heart is the determining factor if one is defiled before God. The Pharisees, then, were wrong: uncleanness had nothing to do with what goes into a man and everything to do with what came out of his heart. Every outward act of sin is preceded by an inward act of choice.[4] Just as, "out of the heart the mouth speaks" (Luke 6.45), so also, "out of the heart the person acts." It is our own heart that defiles us because of the impurity that we allow to reside there and overflow into our lives when we choose sinful things.

We might think again of the basic call to discipleship in Luke 9.22–27. Without rehashing everything already said in chapter 2, this passage also supports the picture of self being the enemy, since self must be denied and crucified daily. The death of self is one of the most fundamental principles of Christianity: self-crucifixion (Gal 2.20); self-sacrifice (Rom 12.1–2); putting self to death (Rom 6.1–14); living a new life, having put to death that which is earthly (Col 3.1–17). Self is the enemy. Self must be done away with.

The Problem of Desire

In addition to the implications against self considered above, the Bible also explicitly identifies self as the problem. Consider what John and James say about the desires of self. The problem is when self takes these desires and turns them into sin.

Desires of the Flesh. John points to the problem of sin being rooted in the desire for things of the world:

Do not love the world or the things in the world. If anyone loves the world, the love of the Father is not in him. For all that is in the world—the desires of the flesh and the desires of the eyes and pride of life—is not from the Father but is from the world. And the world is passing away along with its desires, but whoever does the will of God abides forever. (1 John 2.15–17)

First, it should be clarified that John's reference to "the world" is not about the planet earth or even things that are physical or created. Nor is he referring to things that are what we might call "secular" as opposed to "spiritual." He clearly defines what he means by "the world" when he refers to "all that is in the world" being desires and pride and that "all that is in the world . . . is not from the Father." Clearly, the created world and its created elements *are* from the Father and are to be used and enjoyed. "The world," then, refers to the things that are rebellious and against God; thus, love for God and love for the world are mutually exclusive.

Desire is not, in itself, a sinful thing. Desire alone is morally neutral. In fact, many of the desires we have are hard-wired into us by God; the desire for food, sleep, and sex are part of our human makeup and there is nothing wrong with any of those desires. It is our relationship to those desires that give them a moral quality, whether good or bad. When desire overruns us, self turns it into something it ought not be by idolizing it or obsessing over it. The desire for food turns into gluttony; the desire for sleep becomes slothfulness; the desire for sex becomes adultery, fornication, or other sexual sins.

We often consider this passage as listing three categories of sin. It may, however, be better to see it as one broad category with two subcategories. Throughout the New Testament, "flesh" does not just refer to bodily sins. The flesh is all that is opposed to the Spirit. If that use is applicable here, then the desire of the flesh encompasses all sin, of which are the desire of the eyes (temptations from without) and the pride of life (temptations from within). The lust of the flesh is inclusive and is filled out by the other two. Selfish human desire [i.e., "the flesh"] is stimulated by what the eye sees and expresses itself in outward show.[5]

John does not openly speak of "self," but we cannot read this text without seeing the idea throughout. Who is the one who falls prey to loving the things opposed to God? Who is the one who allows these desires to overrun my life? How can I think of the desires that lead to sin without realizing, again, that I am my own worst enemy?

His Own Desire. The questions we just asked are answered unequivocally in James:

> Blessed is the man who remains steadfast under trial, for when he has stood the test he will receive the crown of life, which God has promised to those who love him. Let no one say when he is tempted, "I am being tempted by God," for God cannot be tempted with evil, and he himself tempts no one. But each person is tempted when he is lured and enticed by his own desire. Then desire when it has conceived gives birth to sin, and sin when it is fully grown brings forth death. (Jas 1.12–15)

This passage takes us back to the problem of making excuses. James issues a clear directive: *don't blame God.* Yet how often do we do this very thing, even though we couch it in other terms. "I'm only human" is an indictment of the One who made us human. "I have a weakness" implies that we were given no option but to sin. God is not to blame for our failings. He is not the enemy. God is the only hope of victory.

More to the point, James makes clear that the problem is self. Temptation arises from "his own desire." Barclay well says, "Every man is a walking civil war … pulled in two directions."[6] We want to be pleasing to God. We want to do the things that God would have us do. But we are pulled the other way by our own desires. Our selfish, fleshly desires are at the root of all sin. As was said in chapter 2, every sin is a manifestation of selfishness. We say to God, "I would rather do what I want to do than what you would have me do." Barclay goes on to say, "Sin would be helpless if there was nothing in man to which it could appeal. If temptation struck no answering chord, then temptation would not be temptation."[7]

Nearly all commentators point out the fishing analogy James uses to make his point. The word "enticed" is from a root that means "bait." The ESV's "lured" may be better rendered "carried away." The image is of a fish swimming happily down a stream when it sees something alluring. Only too late does it discover the hook that drags it away. It is a picture of Satan casting the enticements of sin before us and tempting the desire that is within us—and then hooking us and dragging us away when we bite. But, as James make clear, it is only because we listen to our desires.

This is the first step in the death-cycle of sin. Desire conceives and gives birth to sin which ultimately becomes full-grown death. Desire becomes action (sin); sin produces death. It is similar to the downward spiral of sin that can be seen both in Ephesians 4.17–19 and Romans 1.18–32. In both texts, immorality begins with hardness of heart before turning into ignorance and darkened understanding. From there, the sinner is alienated from the life of God before becoming calloused and giving himself up to every kind of sensuality.[8] This process, from beginning to end, is rooted in self. Notice also how closely the list of wickedness in Romans 1.29–32 parallels Jesus' list of desires in Mark 7.21–23.

It may be helpful here to be reminded that it is not sinful to be tempted. Jesus was tempted. But there are some tender-hearted Christians who may think their ongoing battles with temptation somehow demonstrate a weakness. It is, however, only when we welcome the temptation rather than resisting it that we sin. Douglas Moo is, I think, right in his assessment:

> To be sure, as one develops more and more of a Christian 'mind,' the frequency and power of temptation should grow less. But temptation will be a part of our experience, as it was the experience of the Lord himself (Heb 2.18), throughout our time on earth. Christian maturity is not indicated by the infrequency of temptation but by the infrequency of succumbing to it.[9]

Toward a Solution

What is the solution to the problem of self? The rest of this book will be dealing with some very practical things we can do to overcome temptation, which may help answer that question. Before that, I will suggest three things.

Crucify self. This was the point of chapter 2. It cannot be overstated how essential it is to deny self. We must crucify our fleshly desires and say "no" to ourselves every time self stands against God; self must be put to death.

The key is not merely overcoming a habit or sin, but becoming a new person. As long as we remain the old person "trying to do better," we are doomed to fail, because we cannot exercise iron control over ourselves successfully. We stop sinning and turn from the temptation not to "become a better person," but as part of the process of being a *new,* totally different person.

Remember the transience of desire. John reminds us of this very thing: the sins we find so alluring are transient, but the things of God are destined to eternity (1 John 2.17). The things we desire so much, the things that self would have us do that stand against God are all doomed. They are all passing away. None will endure. We must actively remember that people with a lust that is worldly will surely pass away with the world. Again, Barclay's comment is worth considering:

> The man who attaches himself to the world's aims and the world's ways is giving his life to things which literally have no future. All these things are passing away and none has any permanency. But the man who has taken God as the center of his life has given himself to the things which last forever. The man of the world is doomed to disappointment; the man of God is certain of lasting joy.[10]

We are better than this. What God intends for us and calls us to is better than sin. Satan came to a sinless Eve whom God had made "very good." The preacher said that God made man upright. We have chosen too often to go down a different path, but that is not how God made us; He made us for something better. Nor is it the goal to which He calls us; He calls us to something better. Futility was not the first word used of our world. It does not have to be the last.[11] Futility was not God's goal; it does not have to be our fate.

Now we direct our attention to practical advice regarding overcoming temptation. What are the nuts and bolts to finding success in spiritual warfare? While I do not claim that the next three chapters will solve all of your sin (or that is has solved all of mine), keep reading and you will find a surprisingly simple and eminently practical path to overcoming temptation.

6

TEMPTATION

Before the Battle

Imagine that you have decided to build a house. The day comes when it is time to start building, and without any blueprints, without any budget, without any contractors, and without any expertise in construction—without any forethought whatsoever—you run down to Home Depot to buy some supplies so you can start building. How far would you get in that construction project before you give up or the whole house collapses upon itself?

Imagine you've been hired to coach the local high school football team. The first day of the season comes and you've had no practices, have no coaching staff, and have no team. But you know there are some guys who look like they might be good football players, so you walk the halls looking for people to fill the roster. What sort of success do you think you might have in that first game or any other game that season?

These examples, of course, are absurd. No one would do such a thing. But they serve to emphasize something we all know very well: success requires planning, forethought, and working toward a goal. But if your experience is anything like mine, you probably haven't always faced your spiritual battles with the same forethought. For much of my life, I faced temptations in isolation from each other. I faced each one as it came to me without much preparation. To be honest, I didn't have a whole lot of success.

We realize that we must plan if we want to build a house, we must plan if we want to coach a football team, and, to add one last analogy, we must plan if we are going to war. If we hope to have any success whatsoever, we must plan ahead.

We *are* going to war. And spiritual warfare is no different. The battle for your soul begins long before the fighting ever starts. While we are not being tempted, we should be doing certain things to avoid temptation and steel ourselves so that we will be successful when it comes. Ultimately, the one who will overcome temptation is the one who plans ahead.

Consider the words of David:

> I will ponder the way that is blameless.
> > Oh when will you come to me?
> I will walk with integrity of heart
> > within my house;
> I will not set before my eyes
> > anything that is worthless.
> I hate the work of those who fall away;
> > it shall not cling to me. (Psa 101.2–3a)

In these short few verses, we find three things done by the man after God's own heart in his quest for integrity—things that serve as a good pattern for us to follow and are done long before temptation ever arises.

I Will Ponder the Way That Is Blameless

When was the last time you pondered the blameless way? Far too often we ponder the sinful way. I don't mean that we think sinful things—although we may do that as well—but that we have resigned ourselves to sin. Far too often we say, "We all sin anyway," or "I'm just human," or "I can't help it."

We even cite Scripture to excuse our sinning. After all, "all have sinned and fall short of the glory of God." And, "none is righteous, no, not one." And, of course, "if we say we have no sin, we deceive ourselves, and the truth is not in us."

A constant rehearsal of these verses without a balancing Biblical perspective of the hope of success can lead us to expect that sin is an inevitable part of our daily—maybe even hourly—lives. I have heard many good Christians say things like, "We all sin all the time." We shouldn't! If we all sin all the time, then we probably need to be doing some work on our spiritual lives. Stop sinning all the time!

It is easy to read these verses (that tell us the truth of our situation) and walk away thinking that we have an excuse to go on sinning or that there is no real hope of winning the battle. It can lead to an attitude of resignation: "I'll sin eventually anyway, so there's no point in fighting it now." While we may never come out and say those words, such a defeatist attitude is far too easy to acquire—and it will inevitably lead to defeat; if we have resigned ourselves to sin, we've lost before the battle has even begun.

Although the Bible paints a picture of us all being sinners, all being unholy, and all having failed in this regard, the Biblical concept is not of a defeatist attitude where we hopelessly resign ourselves to sin. Yes, there *is* sin in our lives. That is reality. And yes it is true that we all will sin again. That is reality as well. And we will sin again after that, because we are fallen and we do make mistakes. But understand that there is never any *excuse* for sin. There is never a situation where we *have* to sin. We simply cannot resign ourselves to sinning without even fighting against it.

While the passages above (Rom 3.10, 23; 1 John 1.10) clearly teach that we are all sinners, they do not claim that we must all continue to sin. And certainly they do not suggest that there we should "all sin all the time."

Consider the Bible's answer to this very matter. God calls us to ponder the blameless way.

"The Lord knows how to rescue the godly from trials" (2 Pet 2.9). Is this a defeatist attitude? You get the idea from how some of us talk about sin that this verse says, "The Lord knows how to leave you stranded in temptation because you're just going to sin anyway." No, the Lord knows how to *rescue the godly*, and that means *you*, in *your* battle with temptation, when *you* are struggling, when *you* are face to face with Satan. He knows how to deliver *you*. Take confidence in that. Ponder the blameless way.

"Blessed is the man who remains steadfast under trial, for when he has stood the test he will receive the crown of life, which God has promised to those who love him" (Jas 1.12). We *can* endure temptation. We don't *have to* fall. We don't *have to* sin.

"No temptation has overtaken you that is not common to man. God is faithful, and he will not let you be tempted beyond your ability, but with the temptation he will also provide the way of escape, that you may be able to endure it" (1 Cor 10.13). There is a way of escape that comes with every temptation. God knows your limits. God knows what you can handle and what you cannot. He has promised us that He will not allow us to be in a situation where we have no way out and no choice but to sin. We simply must not resign ourselves to sin before the battle even begins.

The only hope we have of ever overcoming temptation and winning the battle is believing in the promises of God that we can win the battle.

A large part of the problem may be that we make it about *us*—our strength or our weakness or our humanity or our struggles, and what *I* can handle and what *I* can't handle. But ultimately it cannot be about what *I* can or cannot do, nor about who *I* am or what *my* weaknesses are. If I am a Christian, I have been crucified; I have put myself to death. "It is no longer I who live, but Christ who lives in me" (Gal 2.20). God has not made promises about enduring temptation and being delivered from temptation and having a way of escape based on our strength or our ingenuity, but on His power, His grace, and the might of His son who dwells in us.

If, however, I live with a defeatist attitude that sin is an inevitable part of my life, whether I say it or not, I come to the conclusion that "I'll just sin anyway." So I don't fight as hard as I ought to and the power of Christ in me means absolutely nothing. Once I've resigned myself to defeat, I am not really going to fight the temptation.

Ponder the blameless way. Believe that you can win. Have confidence in the strength of Christ, not in your strength.

March Madness, the NCAA Basketball Tournament, is one of my favorite times of the year. What makes it so much fun to watch are the nobody, podunk teams who you have never heard of otherwise playing against a powerhouse university. You look at the rosters, stats, and other measurables and there is no way that that this team can possibly win. But, as they say, games aren't played on paper, and every year, three or four of those little teams with no chance of winning actually win. They don't win because they walk onto the court thinking, "We have no chance to win; we don't even belong on the same court as these guys." The only way they ever win those games is that they believe, in spite of the odds, that they *can* win.

Sometimes reality sets in. Sometimes it doesn't matter that they believe they can win, and they will still lose. But you will never find a team that, believing it will lose, wins. The only way they will ever win is if they think they can.

And our situation is even better than theirs. It is not an "I think I can." It's "I *know* I can" because the power of Christ dwells in us and because God has promised us that we can.

We will never overcome temptation if we approach it with a defeatist attitude. This attitude creates a self-fulfilling prophecy. If we believe that we cannot win, then we *will not* win. If we think sin is an inevitable part of our daily lives, then sin *will be* an inevitable part of our daily lives.

The only way is if we believe that we will win because we *know* we can win, not because of our strength or our ingenuity or anything in us, but because of the One who lives in us and His strength. We must take confidence in the promises of God that He does deliver the godly , it is possible to endure temptation, and that He always provides a way of escape.

Don't ponder the sinful way; ponder the way that is blameless.

I Will Walk with Integrity

One of the amazing things about Bible characters is how easily them seemed to face challenges. Daniel and his friends stood up to kings—the most powerful men in the world—without batting an eye. Joseph, as a slave, refused to compromise his morals in a situation that would cause most seventeen-year-old males to turn into mush. Paul joyfully faced persecution we cannot even imagine and never lost his confidence in the greater glory awaiting him. None flinch. None debate. They just do what they were supposed to do.

How were they able to do this? How could they face temptation in this way? The answer is surprisingly simple: *they decided to.* And then they did it. The way David says it is, "I will walk with integrity of heart within my house." He *chose* to be a person of integrity.

Consider also Daniel: "Daniel resolved that he would not defile himself..." (1.8). He had made a decision that when temptation came, he was going to make the right choice. This is not a decision he made on the spot as he faced temptation; he had already purposed in his heart what he was going to do. In Daniel 1, the matter in question is the king's food that he would not eat, but the principle was pervasive in all of his life. Daniel had already decided long before the temptation ever arose what he would do, or more precisely, what he would *not* do: sin. Daniel's success at overcoming the temptations of his life began with a decision to be righteous. This is true of Daniel's friends and Joseph as well.

In fact, those who are consistently successful in overcoming temptation are so because they decide well in advance of the temptation what they will do. They know ahead of time how they are going to react when the temptation comes.

Daniel's success begins with a decision to be righteous. David's success begins with a decision to choose integrity. The same thing must be true of us if we are going to overcome temptation. The decision must be made before the temptation hits. It is easy to be lackadaisical about temptation when we are not actually being tempted. We might not think about what we will do when the temptation comes because we are not facing it at that moment. Then, out of the blue, Satan pounces and we fail because we have not thought about it, we have not prepared, and we did not know how to handle it when it came. We cannot afford to wait until the encounter to make a decision; if we do so, we will almost surely falter. The moment Satan has us even considering the temptation—deciding, debating the matter, pondering whether the sin is worth it—we have lost our focus on God. We are looking at how *appealing* the sin is and trying to decide whether we want to compromise our morals rather than understanding how *revolting* it truly is and immediately turning away.

Joseph's success in his hour of temptation came not because he stood there deliberating while Potiphar's wife was tugging on his clothes. He knew it was wrong. The decision was made. He left.

The moment we give temptation more thought than an immediate rejection is the moment we open the door to failure.

Actions stem from the heart (cf. Matt 12.34). What we do is directly related to who we are. If the heart is evil, the actions will be evil; if the heart is holy, the actions will be holy. Before temptation arises, we must condition our hearts to purity. Make the decision now while we are not being tempted. Don't give Satan an empty mind to prey upon. Decide now. Force him to change your mind. And then fight with everything you have to prevent him from doing so.

David's decided to walk with integrity "within my house." On some level, then, his was a private decision. Most of us, after all, are really good about being public Christians. Few would openly participate in the things that tempt us privately. But notice that David's decision went beyond public life. It was a decision to be pure, even in the privacy of his home. Beyond that, Paul says that we are to make every *thought* subservient to Christ (2 Cor 10.4).

John Wooden rightly said, "The true test of a man's character is what he does when no one is watching." This is the Biblical standard as well. This is what God calls us to: holiness when only He can see. And that holiness begins with a decision.

I do not want to oversimplify a lifelong struggle or make light of the temptation we face, but there is something startlingly simple about winning our battles. If we are ever to overcome temptation, it begins with the decision that we want to.

I Will Not Set Before My Eyes Anything That Is Worthless

Again, I hesitate to oversimplify this lifelong battle, but on this most fundamental level of what we are to do before temptation, the solution is not complex: don't give up before the fight begins, decide to be good, and now decide *not* to be bad.

David says, "I will not set before my eyes anything that is worthless" and the rest of the psalm could be summarized as the things he will put out of his sight. Obviously, as king, he has a little more prerogative as to how he was going to do that than we do, but the principle ultimately is the same.

Practically speaking, the call in this last phrase is, to the best of our ability, avoid tempting situations. The only way we are ever going to avoid tempting situations is to know ourselves—*honestly* know ourselves. We must see past the self we want others to see to the self we hide from everybody. We must lay ourselves bare before, well, ourselves. We must admit to ourselves what tempts us. And then, as much as we can control it, avoid the people and places that create that temptation.

This, of course, might not be quite as simple as it sounds, but it is still a fundamental principle of what we must be doing before the temptation arises: don't put yourself in a bad situation.

Sometimes we put ourselves in terrible situations, look back, and wonder where our way of escape was. Maybe the way of escape was not to go where we *knew* the temptation would be to begin with! God gave us the way out by giving us the option not to go. And yet we have gone, surrounded ourselves with that, and suddenly we find ourselves sinning because we chose to go where we knew good and well we should not have been.

Temptation is not an extreme sport. Spiritual warfare is not about testing our courage. Battling Satan is not about pushing our limits. Our souls' well-being is not about seeing how much we can handle without going over the edge. The exact opposite is true: stay as far away from it as you can. Do everything within your power to avoid evil.

The preacher says, "He who digs a pit will fall into it" (Ecc 10.8). The principle extends into this topic: if you put yourself in a bad situation, bad things will happen. Keep as far away from temptation as possible.

In a passage on repentance, Ezekiel speaks of casting away from transgression (18.31). The very language of "casting away" from sin speaks of the distance we should keep from what we know tempts us. After all, no one has ever seen a cruise ship "casting off" from shore and never making it out of the harbor, never leaving the view of the folks on the dock. Casting off is getting away from something, leaving it far behind. Likewise, cast off from sin. Cast off from temptation. Don't hang around to get a good look. Keep yourself as far from temptation as you possibly can.

I am sure you have seen a movie where there is a killer in the house and everyone knows it. Everyone, that is, except the girl who is currently safely outside the house. And yet, for some inexplicable reason, she is thinking pretty hard about going back inside. If you are anything like me, you view this scene with frustration over the blatant foolishness: "What are you, an idiot? The killer's in the house. If you go in the house, you're going to die. It doesn't take a genius to figure it out. Everyone in the world—except you, apparently—knows that there's a killer in there."

And you already know what happens. She goes in the house, and she promptly dies. And you think, "This is the most ridiculous thing in the world. How could someone be so stupid?"

I can't help but wonder what my life would look like if it were projected on screen. The killer is sin. The house is temptation. And I am the idiot standing at the door thinking really hard about going back inside. All the rest of the world looks on and says, "What are you, an idiot? You have to know that if you go to that place, spend time with those people, or surround yourself with that environment, you're going to sin. It doesn't take a genius to figure it out. It's obvious to anyone else who is looking." Yet how many times do I go in the house? How many times am I the one who dies in that scene?

There's a killer in the house. Don't go in.

Much of our battle with temptation hinges on what we do before temptation even begins. We have to know that we can win if we are ever going to win. We have to decide to be people of integrity, people of purity, people of holiness. And we must do everything we can not to give Satan an easy victory by going where we know sin waits.

These are simple, obvious principles. Following them, however, does not mean that we will never face temptation or that the battle will always be easy. No matter what we do to avoid it, temptation will find us. But our response to temptation should be planned in advance. You draw up the blueprint first and then you use it while you are building the house. You devise a game plan first and then you use it when you are coaching the game. Don't ever wait for temptation to come before you start fighting—that is the fastest way to lose.

7

TEMPTATION

In the Fray

We concluded the previous chapter with the principle of staying as far away from temptation as possible. This, of course, is sensible advice and a great goal for us as Christians. It is not, however, a foolproof way to overcome every temptation. Regardless of how diligently we work at avoiding tempting situations, we will be tempted. If we do not willingly go to Satan, he *will* actively come after us. Temptation will find us. And it will be, no surprise, tempting. What then?

This is, perhaps, a good place to again issue a reminder: it is not a sin to be tempted. There are times when good, tenderhearted Christians feel a twinge in their conscience when all they have done is been tempted. Understand that the fact of temptation in our lives does not make us sinners; it makes us human. Even Jesus, as we will discuss below, endured temptation.

This chapter discusses principles of what to do in the heat of the battle. It is the practical working out of the second point from the previous chapter. There we discussed making the decision to be pure before temptation arises. Yet it is not enough to theoretically choose integrity but have no concept of what that means in practice. We must know how we will maintain that integrity in the battle. In a sense, then, even this discussion of what we do *during* the temptation is still a discussion of planning in advance.

Here are three simple, practical things that Christians should do during temptation.

Look to Christ

The idea of looking to Christ has a general and a specific application. Generally, it focuses on the idea of prayer. Specifically, it involves considering how He overcame temptation and learning principles from His encounter.

Prayer. The idea of going to Christ in prayer during temptation is rooted Scripture. The author of Hebrews paints a picture of Jesus as the perfect mediator and high priest because He experienced humanity and temptation.

We are probably most familiar with this in terms of Him opening access to God through mediation:

> Since then we have a great high priest who has passed through the heavens, Jesus, the Son of God, let us hold fast our confession. For we do not have a high priest who is unable to sympathize with our weaknesses, but one who in every respect has been tempted as we are, yet without sin. Let us then with confidence draw near to the throne of grace, that we may receive mercy and find grace to help in time of need. (Heb 4.14–16)

But the throne of grace to which we draw is not only the throne of the Father, but the throne of the Son as well. The New Testament regularly portrays Jesus Himself seated on the throne. The author of Hebrews goes on to say that the purpose of a high priest is that "he can deal gently with the ignorant and wayward, since he himself is beset with weakness" (5.2).

He already indicated that "because [Christ] himself has suffered when tempted, he is able to help those who are being tempted" (2.18). The point is that when we are tempted we should go to the One who endured temptation without stumbling. He is there for us for that very reason.

Prayer need not be limited to Christ any more than it should be limited to the Father. During the final hours of Jesus' time with the apostles, He twice speaks of the value of prayer. As He prepares Peter for the temptation to come, Jesus tells him that He has prayed for Peter's faith (Luke 22.32). Shortly after, in Gethsemane, He tells the disciples to pray that they may not enter into temptation (v 40). Their failure in prayer at Gethsemane foreshadows their failure in temptation. Jesus' devotion to prayer foreshadows His devotion to God and successful endurance of the cross.

These scenes should answer anyone who doubts the value of prayer in temptation: Jesus, God in the flesh, prays for others and tells them to pray for the very purpose of overcoming temptation.

We also see prayer considered in relation to spiritual warfare. In Ephesians 6, Paul's discussion of spiritual warfare and the armor of God is concerned with being able to "stand against the schemes of the devil" (v 11), "withstand in the evil day" (v 13), "to stand firm" (v 13), and to "stand" (v 14). Clearly, this is about winning our battles with Satan. Then, after having taken on the whole armor of God, Paul's instruction is not to go out and wage war but to pray—pray at all times with all prayer and supplication with all perseverance for all the saints (v 18). It is too easy, as Stott says, to pray sometimes, with some perseverance, for some of God's people. "But to replace 'some' by 'all' in each of these expressions would be to introduce us to a new dimension of prayer."[1] To that I would add that it would introduce us to a new dimension of overcoming temptation.

The Temptation of Christ. The record of Jesus' victory over temptation in the wilderness is a great text to consider for learning what it takes to overcome temptation. Jesus is the supreme example of overcoming temptation, so there is no better place to look than His success.

> Then Jesus was led up by the Spirit into the wilderness to be tempted by the devil. And after fasting forty days and forty nights, he was hungry. And the tempter came and said to him, "If you are the Son of God, command these stones to become loaves of bread." But he answered, "It is written,
>
> "'Man shall not live by bread alone,
>   but by every word that comes from the mouth of God.'"
>
> Then the devil took him to the holy city and set him on the pinnacle of the temple and said to him, "If you are the Son of God, throw yourself down, for it is written,
>
> "'He will command his angels concerning you,'
>
> and
>
> "'On their hands they will bear you up,
>   lest you strike your foot against a stone.'"
>
> Jesus said to him, "Again it is written, 'You shall not put the Lord your God to the test.'" Again, the devil took him to a very high mountain and showed him all the kingdoms of the world and their glory. And he said to him, "All these I will give you, if you will fall down and worship me." Then Jesus said to him, "Be gone, Satan! For it is written,
>
> "'You shall worship the Lord your God
>   and him only shall you serve.'"

Then the devil left him, and behold, angels came and were ministering to him. (Matt 4.1–11)

While this is not an exhaustive study of that encounter,[2] consider the following basic, practical principles we can learn from Jesus' temptation.

Resisting Satan is more than saying "no" one time. It is easy to over-read James' assurance of Satan's flight at our resistance (Jas 4.7) to indicate that overcoming temptation will be simple: he tempts us, we say "no," he runs away in fear, and that's the end of the matter. In addition to the necessity of understanding that our resistance must be accompanied by the parallel phrase in the following verse (i.e., "Draw near to God, and he will draw near to you"), it is clearly the case in Jesus' temptation that resistance is not a simple "no." Mark's account of the temptation strongly implies that the testing was not limited to the three well-known temptations of Matthew 4 but spanned the entirety of the 40 days in the wilderness (Mark 1.12–13). Luke's account indicates that even after the battle was won, resistance included holding fast when later temptations inevitably arose (Luke 4.13). Satan is not a pushover. Temptation will be a lifelong battle. Every temptation requires continual resistance.

Jesus saw sin for what it is. As previously dicussed, Satan's goal is to make sin appealing, to make us *not* see sin for what it is. If sin came with a flashing neon sign that indicated its abhorrence in the sight of God, its detrimental nature to our soul, and the eternal punishment it brings, it would lose some of its appeal. But Satan tempts us by magnifying what is inherently appealing while disguising its true terrible nature. At every turn in Jesus' temptation, Satan masked the evil. In this encounter, he even quotes Scripture to give faux legitimacy to his claims. Christ overcame because He saw past the lie to the true ugliness of the sin; He saw sin for what it was.

If we are going to be successful at overcoming temptation, we must also see past the lie. Satan is a master salesman—if he let us see sin for what it is, he would have gone out of business long ago—so overcoming temptation requires true spiritual perspective. To the Christian who understands his calling to holiness and self-denial and who clearly sees life through the lens of God's word, sin should not be appealing. We must see the sin as Christ saw it.

Jesus answered temptation with Scripture. One of the greatest powers of Scripture is its ability to terminate temptation. Scripture is the Eternal Truth of God and our enemy is the Father of all Lies; the Father of Lies cannot stand against Eternal Truth.

If we want to see past the lie and not fall prey to Satan's deception, we must reveal it by illuminating it with the truth. We must know our Bibles. We must know what tempts us. We must know what the Bible says about what tempts us. And we must meditate on those things when we are being tempted. Shine the truth on temptation and the lie cannot stand.

It is often remarked that the word of God—the sword of the Spirit—is the only offensive weapon in the arsenal of God's armory. While this is true, we cannot focus on that aspect to the neglect of the value of the sword as a *defensive* weapon. Whether you follow Olympic fencing or have merely seen a pirate movie, you surely are aware of the necessity of a swordsman knowing how to defend himself with his weapon. The same is true in our spiritual warfare. As is said in the quintessential psalm of praise to God's word, "I have stored up your word in my heart that I might not sin against you" (Psa 119.11). In short, Bible study is vital to overcoming temptation. Not only must we know what tempts us, but we must know what God has said about it. With this foundation laid, we will have true spiritual perspective: we can use God's eternal truth to reveal the lies of Satan and stand against him.

Jesus had a plan. I do not mean that He had a specific plan to overcome these specific temptations—though that very well may be true. My point is that His *whole life* was centered on a plan: sinlessness was required so that he could die as a sacrifice for our sin. He knew that every moment, every temptation was *vital* to what He was trying to accomplish.

It is true that no one is going to be saved by our sinless sacrifice and that we have already fallen short of the glory of God, but if we lived our lives with half the desire to stay pure that Jesus had, if we focused our lives with half the intent of not sinning that Jesus had, if overcoming temptation was half as important to us as it was to Jesus' life, we would undoubtedly be more successful in our battles against Satan.

Look to Christians

"Bear one another's burdens," Paul says, "and so fulfill the law of Christ" (Gal 6.2). If this were all that Paul said on the matter, there would be a case that it includes assisting one another in temptation. After all, there is no greater shared burden than temptation; temptation is universal and no one is uniquely tempted. There is no greater blessing that we share than one another. That is why we are here. That is why God, in His infinite wisdom, designed the church to be a group who supports one another in our Christian walk.

But this is not all Paul says on the matter. The preceding verse puts this specifically in the context of the problem of temptation: "Brothers, if anyone is caught in any transgression, you who are spiritual should restore him in a spirit of gentleness. Keep watch on yourself, lest you too should be tempted" (v 1).

I often wonder if there is some kind of reciprocal necessity implied here: what responsibility does this put on me when I am the one being tempted? If my brother has a God-given obligation to bear my burden of temptation, do I have the reciprocal obligation to let him bear it—to share it with him? Of course, this goes against the ideal of American individualism, which has probably crept too deeply into the thinking of God's people: we think we can do it on our own. Perhaps more significantly, it requires a lot of humility to openly face the shame of our sin and admit weakness. But my brother cannot help me in my temptation if I refuse to let him. And so James instructs us this way as well: "Confess your sins to one another and pray for one another" (5.16).

Alcoholics Anonymous is an organization that attracts millions each week to its various local meetings around the world.[3] It is a place where people go in and openly admit the worst of their sins—and are welcomed with open arms by people with the same problem who are willing to devote their lives to helping each other.

The church is also a worldwide group that attracts millions to its weekly meetings. It's a place where people go in, pretend they have it all together and don't struggle with sin—and they are patted on the back by people with the same problem who also don't want to talk about it.

There's something terribly wrong here. Why can we not admit our need to the very people that God put in our lives for our support? Why is it that we have to look to a human institution to see how openness and mutual dependence is supposed to work? Why is it that most Christians would *never* do the sort of thing that is done at AA every week—openly admit their sins to people who are more than willing to help them out?

On some level, this is because we have the false notion of the assembly as a holy place for holy people—and we wouldn't want to offend anyone by talking specifically about what we struggle with. But this is not at all the case. The church is made up of sinners and the assembly is a place for sinners—sinners who know that is what they are and are looking for help to overcome.

Alcoholics Anonymous started one day when its founder realized, "I don't need alcohol; I need another alcoholic." He reached out to a friend who ultimately became the cofounder of the organization. We must come to that same realization: we don't need sin; we need another sinner. We must reach out to each other and together we can stay on that path.

Look to Christianity

Know. Know what you were called to be. It is far too easy to think of sin as inevitable. It's too easy to view temptation from a fleshly perspective rather than a spiritual perspective. It's too easy to nod along with "the spirit is willing but the flesh is weak," while putting all of our emphasis on the latter half of the statement. Instead, we must remember what the Christian life entails. It is helpful in a time of temptation to mediate on the high and noble purpose to which you were called:

> [God] has saved us and called us to a holy calling, not according to
> our works, but according to His own purpose and grace which was
> given to us in Christ Jesus before time began. (2 Tim 1.9)

> His divine power has granted to us all things that pertain to life and godliness, through the knowledge of him who called us to his own glory and excellence, by which he has granted to us his precious and very great promises, so that through them you may become partakers of the divine nature, having escaped the corruption that is in the world because of sinful desire. (2 Pet 1.3–4)

We have been called to something far greater than ourselves, something that has nothing to do with our works, our abilities, or our nature. He has called us to His glory. He has called us to His excellence. He has called us to share in His very nature. And to this high and noble purpose, Paul charges us to "walk worthy of the calling to which you have been called" (Eph 4.1). We must know our calling as Christians, live with it at the forefront of our mind, and never lose focus of it. It is when we lose focus on what we are supposed to be that we believe Satan's lies and become what we should not be.

Grow. Christianity is a growth process. We will not become perfect people overnight, but as we grow our failings will be less frequent. After telling us that we have been given access to become partakers of the divine nature, Peter goes on to say:

> For this very reason, make every effort to supplement your faith with virtue, and virtue with knowledge, and knowledge with self-control, and self-control with steadfastness, and steadfastness with godliness, and godliness with brotherly affection, and brotherly affection with love. For if these qualities are yours and are increasing, they keep you from being ineffective or unfruitful in the knowledge of our Lord Jesus Christ. For whoever lacks these qualities is so nearsighted that he is blind, having forgotten that he was cleansed from his former sins. Therefore, brothers, be all the more diligent to confirm your calling and election, for if you practice these qualities you will never fall. For in this way there will be

richly provided for you an entrance into the eternal kingdom of our Lord and Savior Jesus Christ. (2 Pet 1.5–11)

Peter's "for this very reason" tells us that the purpose of what he will say is about living up to this high and noble calling. We have been called to His glory; we have been called to His excellence; we are to become partakers of the divine nature; we are to escape the corruption that is in the world. Walking worthy of the calling, Peter says, requires growth.

While this book isn't the place for a detailed study of the elements in Peter's list, I want to point out the results of this process. If we have these qualities, we will not be ineffective, we will not be unfruitful; we will be becoming the people that we should be. If we do not have them, we are blind, so blind that we have forgotten that we were cleansed from former sins, which is the first step in a life that turns back to sin. The one who has forgotten what Christ has done, who has forgotten his cleansing, is the one who so quickly returns to wallowing in the mire of sin.

The path to avoiding this fast track to sin is to grow. If we have these qualities, *we will never fall.* Growing as a Christian ensures that we do not forget who we are and that we keep our Christianity and our high calling at the forefront of our mind. The point is not that we will never again sin, but sin will become less and less frequent as we grow closer and closer to God. Ultimately, this is the pathway to heaven, which is what Peter goes on to say specifically in verse 11. Anyone who is growing is securely on the path.

Do. There comes a point where theorizing and meditating must become action. There comes a point where a decision must be made to go out and accomplish what it is that we want to do.

The same thing is true in growing to be the person we want to be. It begins with thought and meditation: "Finally, brothers, whatever is true, whatever is honorable, whatever is just, whatever is pure, whatever is lovely, whatever is commendable, if there is any excellence, if there is anything worthy of praise, *these things think*" (Phil 4.8).[4] It begins by filling your mind with holy, profitable things—those things that align with our high, noble calling and are consistent with our goal of growth. These are the things that lead us to being the people we should be.

But it doesn't stop with thinking: "What you have learned and received and heard and seen in me—*these things do*, and the God of peace will be with you" (Phil 4.9). I wonder how many of our problems come because our faith is too theoretical and not practical enough. There comes a point when we must make a decision and do it. We know all of the right things to do, we think about the right things, we have meditated on the right things. Then, the temptation comes and instead of just doing what we know we need to do, we get swept away in the temptation and sin. There comes a time when we simply have to man up and do what we know we need to do.

The call is to make a decision. Paul says to look at his life, look at what he taught, look at the example of Christ and *do it*. Be the person you are supposed to be.

When the moment of temptation arises, look to Christ for He is our supreme example and our compassionate high priest. Look to Christians, the brothers and sisters who God has given to help with this very problem. Look to Christianity, the high and noble calling. Know it. Grow in it. Do it. And you will never fall.

8

TEMPTATION

After the Fight

The temptation has passed. One of two things has happened: either we have overcome the temptation or the temptation has overcome us. What now? What we do next, of course, largely depends on whether we have succeeded or failed.

Success

I briefly considered in which order to discuss this chapter, whether it was best to open or close with the "good news." The reality, as we will see, is that there is good news even in failure. More significantly, however, it is best to open with success because, as we have said throughout, success *should* be the outcome; failure should be the exception. We should not find ourselves surprised to have succeeded.

Our rate of success might be different at various stages of life. We might not succeed as much in our first years as Christians as we will after 20 years of growth. But as we grow, mature, and become more adept at fighting spiritual battles, success should become more frequent and sin less common. Even John, who twice emphasizes the universality of sin in our lives (1 John 1.8, 10) goes on to say that his purpose in writing is "so that you may not sin" (2.1), indicating confidence in our ability to overcome.

Rejoice. The rejoicing that comes in overcoming temptation is not merely focused on our own success and victory but should primarily be focused on God. Rejoice in the Lord. Praise God for the success that you have had.

Sin does not have to be an inevitable part of your life because our ability to overcome is not about us and our strength; it is about Christ who lives in us, the strength He gives, and the power of God that is in us to overcome temptation. Praise God for that.

The way of escape that Paul speaks of was provided by God. That is the promise: God will give us this way of escape. We saw it, we found it, we used it—but *God* gave it. Praise God for that.

Our brethren to whom we turned for help to bear our burdens in temptation and who helped us overcome are part of the design of God's infinite wisdom. Praise God for such a support group.

Rejoice in the victory over Satan, but rejoice focused on God. It is easy, in our success, to turn our focus inward, and to think about what *we* accomplished. This seems to be the nature of people in general and is certainly the doctrine of our culture: a me-centered, glory-in-what-I-accomplished, look-at-me culture. For Christians, self should always be the last of our focal points. This sort of self-focus, especially in the context of success, can easily lead to arrogance, and suddenly, victory over temptation becomes a temptation itself, and success becomes a stumbling block. Rejoicing should thus be manifest in praise to God.

Such God-focused rejoicing is the natural result of deliverance as depicted in the psalms (cf. Psa 50.15). Psalm 22 depicts David (and ultimately the Messiah) as surrounded by enemies and apparently forsaken by God. All seems hopeless until his prayer for deliverance is answered:

But you, O Lᴏʀᴅ, do not be far off!
    O you my help, come quickly to my aid!
Deliver my soul from the sword,
    my precious life from the power of the dog!
    Save me from the mouth of the lion!
You have rescued me from the horns of the wild oxen!

I will tell your name to my brothers;
    in the midst of the congregation I will praise you:
You who fear the Lᴏʀᴅ, praise him!
    All you offspring of Jacob, glorify him,
    and stand in awe of him, all you offspring of Israel!
For he has not despised or abhorred
    the affliction of the afflicted,
and he has not hidden his face from him,
    but has heard, when he cried to him.

From you comes my praise in the great congregation;
    my vows I will perform before those who fear him.
The afflicted shall eat and be satisfied;
    those who seek him shall praise the Lᴏʀᴅ!
    May your hearts live forever! (vv 19–26)

The one who was crying out for help and feels like he has been forsaken learns that he has not been forsaken at all. God has not despised the affliction of the afflicted; He has not hidden His face from him, but He has heard him who was crying out. And so God is praised when the psalmist is delivered from his enemies because, no matter how it seemed, it turns out that God has not forsaken him (v 24). So the psalmist praises God for His abiding presence and help when surrounded by enemies. Here is the proper focus on the one who has been delivered to-day: praise for God. From this point, the psalmist even goes on to describe the evangelistic effect that such praise will bring as he calls on everyone else to praise God as well (vv 27–31). This is a great picture of the proper focus on praising God, and not only that but also of praise quickly turning into an evangelistic effort: we are rejoicing and praising God and that spills over to a desire for everyone else to join us in praising Him.

Psalm 107 is another great example of praise in time of deliverance. The introduction calls on people of all places to come together and praise God and for the redeemed to speak of their redemption (vv 1–3). The psalm then describes four situations where deliverance is needed: on a desert journey (vv 4–9); from prison (vv 10–16); from sickness (vv 17–22); on a voyage (vv 23–32). Each of these stanzas has a common refrain of plea: "Then they cried to the LORD in their trouble, and he delivered them from their distress" (vv 6, 13, 19, 28). After God's deliverance, each scenario has a common refrain of thanksgiving: "Let them thank the LORD for his steadfast love, for his wondrous works to the children of man!" (vv 8, 15, 21, 31).

The psalm paints a continuous picture of people who are helpless and who are hopeless. They cry out to God. God delivers. What naturally follows such deliverance? Thanksgiving and praise for what God has done.

The psalm concludes with an appeal to consider the steadfast love of the Lord (v 43). Consider what God has done. Consider God's grace, God's mercy, and God's steadfast love. The only thing we can do when we truly consider these things is to praise God, and to rejoice in the deliverance He has provided.

If this is the case for the sort of deliverance described in Psalm 107, how much more so in our victories over temptation? None of the deliverances described in this psalm begin to compare with deliverance from Satan, with the path to victory that

God provides concerning our eternal destiny. That is what God gives us when He gives a way of escape, when the power of His Son leads us to victory over Satan.

Rejoice! Praise God for your victory!

Recommit. Aside from taking credit for victory, the last thing the victor over temptation can afford to do is grow complacent in success. Satan will return. Though he flees when you resist him, he will not stay away forever; as we saw with Jesus' temptation, "he departed from him until an opportune time" (Luke 4.13). He is still a roaring lion seeking after someone to devour (1 Pet 5.8); he is still a dragon cast down from heaven, pursuing God's people in vengeance (Rev 12.13–17).

Our task is to return to the starting point, to humbly recommit to the high and noble calling of holiness, self-denial, and a new life. As we return to the practical lessons of this book, success will help us find them to be easier. We *know* we can win because we just did and can take that confidence into the next battle. Committing to purity and integrity is easier when you have won a battle; it is much harder to rationalize "just one more time" when you have rejected the temptation the last several times. And although we still know that Satan will find us regardless of our efforts, the feeling of victory gives us that much more incentive to keep ourselves out of temptation traps.

Failure

Regardless of how it *should* be, the reality of human existence is that not every encounter with temptation is a successful one. Even though sin is not inevitable and is never excusable, we find ourselves bowing to the flesh far too often. What then?

Repent. Repentance is far more than simply saying, "I'm sorry." It does, of course, involve the acknowledgment of guilt (1 John 1.9), but it is more than just saying the words. In addition to acknowledging guilt, there must be an emotional element. As God demands repentance in the book of Joel, He tells the people to "rend your hearts and not your garments" (2.13a). It is not just the outward act of sorrow (i.e., tearing garments), but an inner distress over sin that God wants. We must be truly moved over our sin. This picture is also reflected in David's prayer of repentance:

> For you will not delight in sacrifice, or I would give it;
>> you will not be pleased with a burnt offering.
> The sacrifices of God are a broken spirit;
>> a broken and contrite heart, O God, you will not despise.
> (Psa 51.16–17)

This is what God wants in repentance: an inward moving of the heart back toward Him.

This leads to the last part of repentance. While the emotional element is necessary, repentance is not mere emotional reaction either. It is not just sorrow in general but sorrow that drives us back to God. It is *changing*: acknowledging guilt, being moved by sin, and changing the person we are. The sorrow experienced must be godly sorrow, which results in the true character of repentance: a changed life: "Godly grief produces a repentance that leads to salvation without regret, whereas worldly grief produces death" (2 Cor 7.10).

The classic example of the difference in these two sorts of grief is seen in Peter and Judas. Each betrayed Jesus. Each felt sorry for what he did and was emotionally moved. The difference between worldly grief and godly grief, between self-centered emotion and God-centered emotion, is clearly exemplified. Judas felt worldly grief and killed himself; Peter felt godly sorrow, repented, and rejoined the cause of Christ. This repentance, this changed life, leads to salvation:

> When a wicked person turns away from the wickedness he has committed and does what is just and right, he shall save his life. Because he considered and turned away from all the transgressions that he had committed, he shall surely live; he shall not die. …Repent and turn from all your transgressions, lest iniquity be your ruin. Cast away from you all the transgressions that you have committed, and make yourselves a new heart and a new spirit. Why will you die, O house of Israel? For I have no pleasure in the death of anyone, declares the Lord GOD; so turn, and live. (Ezek 18.27–28, 30b–32)

Repentance leads to salvation. It is casting away from transgression, defined here as having a new heart and a new spirit, the same thing Paul speaks of in Ephesians 4. Put off the old man, be renewed, and put on the new man (vv 22–24).

Rejoice. The penitent one should then turn to rejoicing. We might not naturally think of rejoicing as something done in the context of having failed a temptation. The context, however, is not in having failed but in having been forgiven and having a God who is so willing to forgive over and over and over again. David's psalm recounting the blessing of forgiveness ends with this very imperative: "Be glad in the LORD, and rejoice, O righteous, and shout for joy, all you upright in heart!" (32.11).

Rejoice that we serve a God who is so forgiving. God's forgiveness is, in fact, at the very nature of His character. The Joel passage cited above goes on to say, "Return to the LORD your God, for he is gracious and merciful, slow to anger, and abounding in steadfast love; and he relents over disaster" (2.13b). Jonah is upset that God has spared the Assyrians and negatively cites this same trait as his complaint and motivation for running from God: "…for I knew that you are a gracious God and merciful, slow to anger and abounding in steadfast love, and relenting from disaster" (4.2).

And consider the following:

> For you, O Lord, are good and forgiving,
> abounding in steadfast love to all who call upon you. (Psa 86.5)

> But you, O Lord, are a God merciful and gracious,
> slow to anger and abounding in steadfast love and faithfulness.
> (Psa 86.15)

> The Lord is merciful and gracious,
> slow to anger and abounding in steadfast love. (Psa 103.8)

> The Lord is gracious and merciful,
> slow to anger and abounding in steadfast love. (Psa 145.8)

> They refused to obey and were not mindful of the wonders that you
> performed among them, but they stiffened their neck and appointed
> a leader to return to their slavery in Egypt. But you are a God ready
> to forgive, gracious and merciful, slow to anger and abounding in
> steadfast love, and did not forsake them. (Neh 9.17)

The historical context of this last example in Nehemiah is Numbers 14. The people have rejected Moses and God's way and want to choose a new leader to return to Egypt. God is ready to wipe them out, but Moses intercedes for them in prayer. What Moses says in that prayer is the very same thing: "The Lord is slow to anger and abounding in steadfast love…" (Num 14.18).

This terminology is so frequent because this is the very nature of God, as spelled out clearly in Exodus 34. There, Moses has requested to see the glory of God. God's manifestation of His glory to Moses was, "The LORD, the LORD, a God merciful and gracious, slow to anger, and abounding in steadfast love and faithfulness..." (Exod 34.6). He then elaborates more about His character, but the first thing is the refrain that shows up so frequently throughout the Old Testament. This is who God is: a forgiving God. This, more than anything, is what we need to know about God because we are a people who are lost in sin without Him. And we are a people who, even though it is inexcusable, are prone to sin again and again.

We often get hung up talking about big, impressive aspects of God's character—things like omnipotence, omnipresence, omniscience, and His eternal nature are our focus. But when God revealed Himself to Moses and when Jesus revealed God to us, it was the humble nature of His character—His selflessness and forgiveness—that was emphasized. And this was the hope (or dread, in Jonah's case) of forgiveness for all who would repent. We should likewise make this our emphasis in talking about God, for it is what we need the most: His omni-benevolence, omni-forgiveness, omni-patience, and -mercy, and -steadfast love. He is not quick to anger but willing to forgive. And what can we do but praise Him? Rejoice for who He is.

Review. Remember the statement about the penitent one in Ezekiel 18: "He considers his transgressions." When was the last time we really *thought* about our sin, what it is, and what it means? We have all heard parents tell a disobeient child, "Go to your room and think about what you've done." While a parent may say that for a variety of reasons, it is good advice for sinners as well: go think about what we have done—not to vaguely say, "We're sorry for the sins we commit," but to truly give thought to sin, to consider the magnitude of sin.

Thinking about past sin does not, of course, mean wallowing in self-pity and regret but positively thinking about the true nature of sin. It is a by-product of godly sorrow. Note that Paul's commendation of the Corinthians' forgiveness speaks to the range of emotion shown in a truly changed life: "For see what earnestness this godly grief has produced in you, but also what eagerness to clear yourselves, what indignation, what fear, what longing, what zeal, what punishment! At every point you have proved yourselves innocent in the matter" (2 Cor 7.11).

While we cannot know exactly how each of these emotions manifested itself in Corinth, we understand how they might find expression in our lives: *earnest* to make everything right; *eager* to clear ourselves; *indignant* with ourselves because of what we've done; *fearful* because of the state of our relationship with God; *longing* to restore that relationship; *zealous* to make it right again with God and others; and determined not to make the same mistake again. This is the result of considering transgression, and it only comes from giving real thought to sin.

The realization of the magnitude of sin that produces godly sorrow ultimately leads us to considering the sin from a very practical perspective: how we will not sin that way again. This principle is why coaches study and show their players film of past games. It allows them to see the things they did wrong—and not just to see them, but to learn from those mistakes and ensure they are not repeated.

We can do the same. When we sin, we should not just repent and give it no more thought. Consider transgression. Review what went wrong. Think about what led to the temptation and caused the sin. Find where the way of escape was that wasn't seen or intentionally ignored. Take time to see through Satan's lies. We must learn from our mistakes so that they are not repeated; if we don't, they surely will be.

CONCLUSION

Perhaps the most surprising aspect of Jacob's wrestling match with God is that the text says he prevailed (Gen 32.28). At best, Jacob fought to a draw. Even then, it was *his* hip that was dislocated and *he* was the one compelled to give up his name. Jacob clearly did not win the fight.

Jacob did, however, win. He won by losing. His struggle was not with God but with himself. Once he stopped clinging to self and started clinging to God, he could admit who he was and be changed. Curtis says, "God struggles with Jacob, and in the process Jacob prevails—not in the sense that he overcomes God, but in the sense that by recognizing his dependence on God he is now able to receive the promise."[1] Ross adds,

> What he had surmised for the past 20 years now dawned on him—he was in the hands of One against whom it is useless to struggle. One wrestles on only when he thinks his opponent can be beaten. With the crippling touch, Jacob's struggle took a new direction. With the same scrappy persistence he clung to his Opponent for a blessing. His goal was now different. Now crippled in his natural strength, he became bold in faith.[2]

The sun will not rise on us until we give up self. As long as we cling to self instead of clinging to God for a blessing, we are residents of the darkness.

Finally, it should be said that if we want to overcome temptation, we must *want* to overcome temptation. Our desires to do so cannot be mere lip service. It cannot be a façade we put on to go to church. We cannot merely say the right things, do the right worship acts, hang out with the right people, sing the right songs, and pray the right prayers, but deep down—if we are honest with ourselves—we know that we do not really want to give up whatever secret sin we have hidden away in our hearts.

We must truly *want* to give up sin. If we want to cling to it on any level, we will never overcome it because we have not truly denied ourselves. We have not crucified the old man. As long as we are dragging him around with us, Satan has us in the palm of his hand.

The question that faces us as we consider our holy calling and our daily battles with Satan is one that has to do with desire. How much do we desire a relationship with God? How much do we want to grow into the image of our Father? How much do we want to be with Him eternally? Are we willing to give up the sin we find so appealing?

That is the call of Christianity: to put self to death, to truly sacrifice everything, and to give it all up for God because any amount of self is too much.

The reward for heeding the call: daybreak.

NOTES

Introduction

[1] For a fuller exposition of Genesis 32, see my *The Growth of the Seed* (Chillicothe: DeWard Publishing, 2007), 323–334.

Chapter 2 – The Call: Self-Denial

[1] C.S. Lewis, *The Weight of Glory and Other Addresses*, rev. ed. (New York: Macmillan, 1980), 3–4.

[2] William Barclay, *The Gospel of Matthew*, Vol. 2, rev. ed. (Philadelphia: The Westminster Press, 1975), 151.

[3] Dene Ward, *Flight Paths: A Devotional Guide for Your Journey* (Chillicothe: DeWard Publishing, 2010), 467.

[4] Leon Morris, *The Gospel According to Luke: An Introduction and Commentary* (Grand Rapids: Eerdmans, 1980), 170.

[5] Richard N. Longenecker, *Galatians* (Waco: Word, 1990), 92.

[6] Ben Witherington III, *Paul's Letter to the Romans: A Socio-Rhetorical Commentary* (Grand Rapids: Eerdmans, 2004), 284–285.

[7] I found Leon Morris' comments particularly insightful in bringing out some of these points of emphasis. Paraphrases of his thoughts are found throughout this section. *The Epistle to the Romans* (Grand Rapids: Eerdmans, 1988), 244–259.

Chapter 3 – The Call: New Life

[1] Much of my thinking in this chapter is influenced by F. F. Bruce and William Barclay. Paraphrases of their thoughts are found throughout this section. F. F. Bruce, *The Epistles to the Colossians, to Philemon, and to the Ephesians* (Grand Rapids: Eerdmans, 1984), 131–160. William Barclay, *The Letters to The Philippians, Colossians, and Thessalonians* (Philadelphia: The Westminster Press, 1959), 176–191.

[2] Douglas J. Moo, *The Letters to the Colossians and Philemon* (Grand Rapids: Eerdmans, 2008), 264.

[3] Ralph P. Martin, *Ephesians, Colossians, and Philemon* (Louisville: John Knox Press, 1991), 126.

[4] Bruce, 160.

Chapter 4 – The Enemy: Satan

[1] Isaiah 14.4–21 and Ezekiel 28.1–19 *might* allude to the fall of Satan and thus give us further information. This is not certain and is clearly not the main point of those prophecies, which are against the kings of Babylon and Tyre, respectively.

[2] For a fuller exposition of these verses and the sources that most affected my thinking on this text, see *The Growth of the Seed*, 59–63.

[3] My thinking on this topic was profoundly impacted by "The Role of Satan in the Bible," an unpublished essay by Phil Roberts.

Chapter 5 – The Enemy: Self

[1] Derek Kidner, *The Message of Ecclesiastes* (Downers Grove: Intervarsity, 1976), 73.

[2] Franz Delitzsch, *Proverbs, Ecclesiastes, Song of Solomon* (1866–91; repr., Peabody: Hendrickson Publishers: 2001), 215.

[3] Inclusio is a figure of speech where a section of text begins and ends with the same sentence, phrase, key word, or concept. Framing the entire section in such a way gives the text a common theme and sense of unity. For simple introduction to the use of inclusio in Hebrew poetry see, for example, Tremper Longman III, *How to Read the Psalms* (Downers Grove: Intervarsity, 1988), 107–108.

[4] William Barclay, *The Gospel of Mark,* rev. ed. (Philadelphia: The Westminster Press, 1975), 173.

[5] I. Howard Marshall, *The Epistles of John* (Grand Rapids: Eerdmans, 1978), 145–146.

[6] William Barclay, *The Letters of James and Peter* (Philadelphia: The Westminster Press, 1960), 58.

[7] Ibid., 61.

[8] For a fuller exposition of this idea and a comparison of the two texts in more detail, see John R. W. Stott, *The Message of Ephesians* (Downers Gorve: Intervaristy, 1979), 174–178.

[9] Douglas J. Moo, *The Letter of James* (Grand Rapids: Eerdmans, 2000), 76.

[10] William Barclay, *The Letters of John and Jude*, rev. ed. (Philadelphia: The Westminster Press, 1976), 59.

[11] Kidner, 73.

Chapter 7 – Temptation: In the Fray
[1] John R. W. Stott, *The Message of Ephesians* (Downers Grove: Intervarsity, 1979), 283–284.

[2] For that, see, for example, Phil Roberts, "The Temptation of Jesus," *Leaving a Mark: The Lectures of Phil Roberts,* ed. Nathan Ward (Temple Terrace: FC Press, 2013), 99–117.

[3] My first encounter with this illustration was in the writing of Philip Yancey, e.g., *Church: Why Bother?* (Grand Rapids: Zondervan, 1998), 48–52.

[4] This translation (and the one to follow) is modified from the ESV to reflect the parallel nature of Paul's admonitions. Emphasis added.

Conclusion
[1] Edward M. Curtis, "Structure, Style and Context as a Key to Interpreting Jacob's Encounter at Peniel," *Journal of the Evangelical Theological Society* 30 No. 2 (1987): 135.

[2] Allen P. Ross, "Studies in the Life of Jacob, Part 2—Jacob at the Jabbok, Israel at Peniel," *Bibliotheca Sacra* 142 (1985): 350.

Also By Nathan Ward

The Growth of the Seed
Notes on the Book of Genesis

A study of the book of Genesis that emphasizes two primary themes: the development of the Messianic line and the growing enmity between the righteous and the wicked. In addition, it provides detailed comments on the text and short essays on several subjects that are suggested in, yet peripheral to, Genesis. 537 pages. $19.99 (PB).

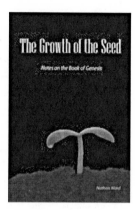

Beneath the Cross
Essays amd Reflections on the Lord's Supper
Jady S. Copeland and Nathan Ward (editors)

The Bible has much to say about the Lord's Supper. Almost every component of this memorial is rich with meaning—meaning supplied by Old Testament foreshadowing and New Testament teaching. The Lord's death itself is meaningful and significant in ways we rarely point out. In sixty-nine essays by forty different authors, Beneath the Cross explores the depths of symbolism and meaning to be found in the last hours of the Lord's life and offers a helpful look at the memorial feast that commemorates it. 329 pages. $14.99 (PB); $23.99 (HB).

Hard Core: Defeating Sexual Temptation with a Superior Satisfaction
Jason Hardin

So many—men and women included—are being
slaughtered in their struggle with sexual sin. Individual lives, marriages, children, influences for good,
ministries of gospel preachers, and entire congrega-
tions of the Lord's people are being seriously impacted. If we are going to win this battle, we must strike
at the root of the problem. We must sound the call
for righteous warfare. We must dedicate ourselves to
hardcore holiness and fight sexual temptation with a
superior satisfaction. 106 pages. $7.99 (PB).

Invitation to a Spiritual Revolution
Paul Earnhart

Few preachers have studied the Sermon on the
Mount as intensively or spoken on its contents so
frequently and effectively as the author of this work.
His excellent and very readable written analysis
appeared first as a series of articles in Christianity
Magazine. By popular demand it is here offered in
one volume so that it can be more easily preserved,
circulated, read, reread and made available to those
who would not otherwise have access to it. Foreword
by Sewell Hall. 173 pages. $9.99 (PB).

Penny Sue the Pure-Hearted
Serena DeGarmo

What did Jesus mean when He asked us to be pure in
heart? Penny Sue will find out when she comes face-
to-face with a new girl at school who is rather prickly.
Why is this person so difficult to get to know? Will
Penny Sue be able to make friends with a girl who
might be bad? Some things aren't always what they
seem. See how God helps Penny Sue and see what
happens with these two unlikely friends. 32 full-
color pages. $7.99 (PB).

In the Garden with God
Dene Ward

Dene Ward and her husband Keith have gardened for nearly 40 years, which has shown her why God's prophets and preachers, including Jesus, used so many references to plants and planting—it's only natural. Join her for a walk in the garden with God. 142 pages. $9.99 (PB).

Soul Food: Lessons from Hearth to Heart
Dene Ward

Cooking has always been a part of Dene Ward's life. She grew up in a house where they were always feeding someone and followed that same path as a wife and mother. On the table, she has always offered a nourishing meal; she now offers this collection to feed your souls, lessons from her hearth to your heart. 148 pages. $9.99 (PB).

For a full listing of DeWard Publishing Company books, visit our website:

www.deward.com

CPSIA information can be obtained at www.ICGtesting.com
Printed in the USA
BVOW080413310513

322064BV00001B/6/P